# Holding Me Together

# Holding Me Together

✦

## Essays and Poems

*Written 1983–2005*

## By Duane Simolke

iUniverse, Inc.

New York  Lincoln  Shanghai

# Holding Me Together
### Essays and Poems

iUniverse books may be ordered through booksellers or by contacting:

iUniverse
2021 Pine Lake Road, Suite 100
Lincoln, NE 68512
www.iuniverse.com
1-800-Authors (1-800-288-4677)

ISBN-13: 978-0-595-36673-6 (pbk)
ISBN-13: 978-0-595-81095-6 (ebk)
ISBN-10: 0-595-36673-2 (pbk)
ISBN-10: 0-595-81095-0 (ebk)

Printed in the United States of America

# *Contents*

# Dedication, Acknowledgement, and Notes

The author wishes to dedicate this book to all the people mentioned in his poem "Editing." He also wishes to thank the reviewers at FanStory.Com and all the other people who support him and encourage him in his writing.

This book contains many quotes from the King James Bible. The use of non-standard spellings within some of those quotes is consistent with how they appear in that translation.

# Part One:
# Reactions to Homophobia,
# An Essay

# REACTIONS TO HOMOPHOBIA: INTRODUCTION

We all know the situation: somebody—hands on hips, fingers pointed, or fists clenched—uses at least one of the tired clichés that follow below. Since we know what to expect, I wanted to offer my reactions. All of those reactions come after a particular quote. I realize that other gays might not offer the same reactions, since they might not hold my views. Still, coming up with those reactions helped me work through countless issues, and I hope my responses will empower, educate, and edify many other people, regardless of their views or their sexual orientation.

Please note that I try to avoid using the words "straight" and "normal" for heterosexuals in this essay, because both terms suggest superiority over gays, by relegating gays to the status of "crooked" and "abnormal." In speech, attempts at such distinctions become awkward, but I try to make those distinctions when writing.

Earlier versions (or excerpts) of "Reactions" appeared in various publications and on numerous Web sites. I finished revising this book and this essay in 1999, and wrote a revised version of both in 2005. Certain laws and legislation that I mention herein might have changed since I finished this version, as they change constantly. Hopefully, we can help them change for the better.

Some people say that writing an essay called "Reactions to Homophobia" means I'm calling them homophobes, when they are merely expressing concern for people who need saving (i.e., need to be clones of themselves). If I wrote an essay called "Reactions to Racism," would the same people say I'm calling them racists, or would they realize that I just want to challenge views that I see as racist and as hurtful? Those same people probably wouldn't say I'm calling anyone anti-religious if I wrote an essay called "Reactions to Religious Persecution." All too often, condemning or silencing someone else's group seems fine.

I'm not calling people names; I'm just trying to help people stop hating themselves and each other. Ultimately, though, I wrote this essay as a way of helping with my own journey of challenging internalized homophobia. Just writing it helped me a great deal with accepting myself and others, and I've heard from countless people who said it helped them the same ways.

Please don't disregard this essay by labeling it as "liberal." People who want to avoid logical argument will often scream catch terms like that and "political correctness" whenever confronted with complicated discussions. Using those terms supposedly excuses them from exploring issues. Some people will even use the word "atheism" for rhetorical bullying; they imply—or even state—that anyone who disagrees with their views about a particular issue obviously does not believe in God. We all know, however, that people within every group or label disagree with each other. People are complicated.

Many people, myself included, find all political titles inadequate for describing themselves. I vote according to the records, views, and credentials of the individual candidates, instead of letting the leaders of any political party or leaning decide my vote for me. Both major parties constantly betray the gay community, using us as scapegoats for the problems they rarely confront directly: violent crime, heterosexual divorce, teen pregnancy, etc. Some Republicans even blame us for earthquakes and floods. Both parties maintain the absurd tradition of letting mostly white male heterosexuals control a diverse society, so it should surprise no one that our leaders continue to fail that diverse society, instead of uniting it or tapping into the advantages of its diversity.

I'm asking you to please look beyond those categories and try to view gay issues in new ways. Throughout this long essay, I will often use the term "many gays" in place of "gays." After all, we are not some collective mind. Our views conflict with each other, just as the views of heterosexuals conflict with each other. We do not all hold the same views, values, or beliefs. We are individual human beings. Just like you, we are all complicated, but simply human.

Thank you for taking the time to read my work, even if you don't agree with it.

# "UNLIKE GAY PEOPLE, I DON'T TELL PEOPLE WHAT MY WIFE AND I DO IN BED."

Are you only heterosexual during sex? If so, do virgins lack a sexual orientation? Calling myself gay refers to who and what I am, not just what I do in bed.

If calling myself gay means saying what I do in bed, then mentioning your heterosexual marriage means saying what you do in bed. The same goes for when heterosexuals announce their marriages and anniversaries in the newspaper; when they ask about or talk about girlfriends and boyfriends while at school; when they refer to their spouses or other romantic interests while at work; when they put each other's pictures on office desks; when they hold hands in public; when they bring their significant others to job-related parties; when they try to set up one of their coworkers on a blind, heterosexual date; and when they assume they can always visit relatives as a couple. After all, those actions or references point to one's sexual orientation.

Unsatisfied with all that flaunting of heterosexuality, they even wear engagement rings or wedding rings to signify their heterosexual status, and they love for people to compliment those rings. Coworkers and family members will often ask personal questions regarding one's marital status, dating preferences, etc., but then say "You should keep that to yourself" if a gay person answers those questions truthfully.

Reality includes diversity, like it or not. Even if I decided to abstain from sex the rest of my life, that wouldn't change who I am or who I love.

Imagine that, at age thirteen, you develop a red mark on your shoulder. You keep it secret from everyone, because you always hear that red-marked people spread disease, destroy families, hate God, and go to Hell. You hear rumors about your people everywhere you go, but you wonder why none of those rumors seem to accurately represent you. Still, you dare not speak out, because of what happened to the other red-marked people you've encountered. One's parents kicked her out at age fourteen, another's classmates beat him nearly to death without getting into any trouble, and another lost her job after someone yanked her shirt down far enough for everyone to see the mark. You live in fear of speaking out, but you know that failing to speak out will mean not only living a lie but also condemning others like yourself to a life of fear and discrimination. Hiding and not hiding both seem like terrible choices. Welcome to the closet.

Countless heterosexual males (teen and up) go around telling each other what they did in bed, with whom they did it, and (quite often) how impressed she was.

Undoubtedly, some of those fellows exaggerate. Whatever the case, heterosexuals in general aren't any more or less discrete about their sexual activity than gays in general. And, unlike many heterosexual males, most lesbians certainly wouldn't walk up to people they barely know and say something like "Man, I bagged me a hot bitch last night."

# "THEY CAN BE GAY, AS LONG AS THEY HIDE IT."

Should we accept left-handed people, as long as they use their right hand; green-eyed people, as long as they wear blue contact lenses; people of color, as long as they use skin-bleaching agents? Why teach people to hate themselves, betray themselves, and live a lie?

Coming out of the closet allows gays to live more honestly, and it allows our heterosexual acquaintances to see gay human beings, instead of just hearing gay stereotypes. Hopefully, those heterosexuals will less likely resort to discrimination and hate crimes, after seeing gays as part of their circle of relatives, coworkers, leaders, and friends. Heterosexuals often don't realize that some of the people they know are gay. If everyone realized it, everyone would probably start thinking of gays as human beings.

Gays won't all stand out or fulfill the gay stereotypes that supposedly make us identifiable. The few gays who can't hide their orientation thus become our representatives: those identified in and out of the gay community as the flaming queen and the bull dyke, not to mention those with so much money that they can afford to tell everyone everything. All of those people contribute to the diversity of the gay community, but no one represents or epitomizes all gays.

Without realizing my orientation, certain nongays will sometimes tell me something crazy like, "I can spot a faggot from a mile off," or "I don't know any gay people." I probably should find those remarks annoying or even offensive, but I actually find the irony of the situation amusing. We're everywhere, and we need to stop lying about it. We leave other gays feeling isolated and hopeless when we refuse to come out to anyone; realizing that we aren't isolated gives us hope and has even prevented many gays from committing suicide.

Yes, we are all over the place, but many of us remain incognito. Some of your coworkers, friends, or relatives are probably closeted gays. People tend to assume that everyone is heterosexual, just as they tend to assume that everyone is right-handed and that everyone has average hearing abilities. Actually, many people are gay, left-handed, or hearing impaired; some people are even all three. Why should we not clear up misconceptions?

Why should we cause the people we know—and especially the people we love—to believe something untrue about us? Isn't that dishonest? Won't it lead to embarrassing situations that will require us to not only cover up but also actively lie? Won't it hurt others if they find out we've been deceiving them?

Assumptions might cause a teacher to put a left-handed student in a right-handed desk and put a hard-at-hearing student in the back of the classroom. That teacher will hardly be the last person to make harmful assumptions about those people. Clearing up those assumptions will help that teacher and those students. The same goes for gays and the people in their lives who want to find them dates with the opposite sex or invite them to bring "a significant other" to a place that won't welcome their significant other.

Imagine that Susan loves spending time with Joe and his other "best friend" Kevin, not knowing that "best friend" is a euphemism in Kevin's case. She falls in love with Joe, a follower of the notion that gays need to "hide it." Think of the pain she must endure because societal pressures convinced Joe that he should lie. Susan never bothers looking for someone else, because she thinks Joe will eventually fall in love with her. Joe's parents go through life thinking that Joe will one day marry Susan and give them grandchildren. Kevin wishes that Joe would stop hiding their relationship from everyone, as if Joe were ashamed of him. Joe really loves Kevin, and Joe realizes that he could never fully return Susan's romantic love. Should he keep his sexual orientation to himself?

Many gays cannot come out, because of various circumstances. Many others simply choose not to, which is their right. However, it seems cruel to force all the others to remain silent.

# "If a normal guy or a white guy gets beat up, hate crimes laws can't help him. That isn't fair."

It also isn't true. We can assume that "normal guy" means "heterosexual male" to you and then proceed with the scenario.

If someone beats up or murders someone else for being heterosexual, that constitutes a hate crime on the basis of sexual orientation. For being white, a hate crime based on race. For being Baptist, Jewish, or Mormon, a hate crime based on religion. Someone who assaults or kills someone else for reasons that are all unrelated to the victim's group(s) is not committing a hate crime, even if the victim is an African American Jewish drag queen with a British accent and a Cuban cigar.

Hate crimes can target anyone, so hate crimes laws can benefit and protect everyone. They also encourage everyone to not express their views through violence or the threat thereof. Murder is not a part of free speech. People can hate anyone or everyone; no law can change how people feel inside. Besides, the Constitution encourages free expression. However, it does so with respect to the rights of others. Harassing, assaulting, or killing people is not a part of the Constitution, even if those vile acts stem from one's religious or patriotic beliefs.

Many states offer clear hate crimes laws, and those laws help the legal system in prosecuting the perpetrators. However, some states rely on vague, unenforceable hate crimes laws that fail to mention the hate biases of the perpetrators—most commonly, race, ethnicity, religion, sexual orientation, and country of origin. Some states omit sexual orientation from that list, which both implies that it's all right to kill people of a hated sexual orientation and ignores the fact that gays become frequent targets of hate crimes. Some states lack hate crimes laws. Why?

The main reason is the "special rights" lie, as if not being assaulted or murdered were a special right. However, I often hear some other popular arguments. They might sound rational on the surface, but maybe not below the surface.

One argument says that motivation is irrelevant in cases of violent crimes. Oddly, this argument often comes from elected officials who deal with the legal system every day. Those people know that motivation plays a vital role in violent crime trials. It decides who is guilty, what charges the jury will consider, and what punishment the guilty will receive. Was it a crime of passion? Was it negligent homicide? Did the accused have a vendetta against the victim? Did the accused want to teach the victim a lesson or even see the victim dead? Those questions, like countless others asked during violent crime trials, revolve around motivation. How can motivation suddenly stop mattering when it comes to hate crimes?

Hatred is the motivation—hatred for a particular group, taken out on an individual human being. Hate crimes stand out in that the accused attacks the entire group that way, perhaps not even thinking of the person. Therefore, the accused will probably want to continue with more hate crimes. After all, the group still exists after the murder of that individual. We need to deal with the uniqueness of this kind of crime and this kind of perpetrator. So, yes, motivation matters.

Secondly, many people claim that existing laws cover hate crimes. But that leads back into the situations I just covered. We have separate laws based on intent. We even have separate laws based on age group (child abuse, etc.) and relationship (domestic violence, etc.). For years, Texas even maintained a separate law protecting oil derricks from attack, but not a clear and enforceable hate crimes law; fortunately, one eventually passed. While most people would prefer to avoid new laws, it seems that they would want to make an exception when those laws target violent crimes.

The existing laws often fail to provide justice in hate crimes cases—especially anti-gay hate crimes, where the perpetrator sometimes receives more sympathy than the victim. In the past, a man who murdered a gay person needed only to shout a few Bible verses and claim that his manhood felt threatened, and many juries would suddenly see him as heroic or a victim of circumstance; at least that defense, known as "gay panic" or "homosexual panic," eventually became less acceptable in the United States. In cases like the one I just gave, a hate crimes law could have reminded the jury that the feelings and religious beliefs of the accused could not give him the right to murder someone.

Another argument claims that including gays in hate crimes laws encourages homosexuality. With some exceptions, gays tend to believe that they can neither choose nor change their orientation, no matter what claims we hear to the contrary. Still, let us assume that gays can choose or change their sexual orientation and that we should exclude "sexual orientation" from hate crimes laws on that basis.

Christianity easily qualifies as the most popular religion in America. People can choose or change their religious affiliations. We could leave out religious liberty protections in such a way as to pressure Muslims and Jews to convert to Christianity, or pretend to do so. We could phrase any such laws so that they can only protect Christians, and change all tax exemption laws so that they only help Christian organizations and Christian places of worship.

That scenario might appeal to some people, but it doesn't sound very American. We came to America (at least in part) to claim religious freedom, not to prevent it. And keep in mind that leaving "religion" off the list means that Christians will lose hate crimes protections. Also keep in mind that certain individuals in one Christian denomination will sometimes commit violence against Christians for belonging to another Christian denomination; "religion" in a hate crimes statute would still cover those scenarios.

We need to make liberty and justice apply to everyone, so the Constitution will remain more than simply a piece of paper. When we say, "Let's mention religion within the hate crimes law," we don't encourage or discourage any particular religious belief. We simply encourage justice and freedom, while discouraging discrimination and violence. The same goes with including the term "sexual orientation." Even if gays could or should choose not to be gay, we still need laws protecting them, and everyone else, from violence.

Protection from violence and harassment is not a "special right." It's a civil right. It's an American right. And it's simply right. Of course we can't legislate hatred away, and we shouldn't try to control other people's thoughts, but we can pass and enforce strict laws that will reduce violent crime in America. It makes sense that all hate crimes should be among the targets of law enforcement agencies and lawmakers who want to (as they say) "get tough" on violent crime.

The FBI's Web site (http://www.fbi.gov/) shows that attacks against gays continue. In cases where the crime leads to death, the attacker often inflicts enough wounds to kill one person several times over, or a group of people works together to randomly target one gay person. While we might like to pretend that such events only happened to Matthew Shepard in Wyoming, they actually happen all over America and all over the world. Here in America, groups of people sometimes even visit largely gay neighborhoods for the sole purpose of bashing someone, but that activity receives little or no attention outside the gay media.

Sadly, many anti-gay hate crimes go unreported, because the survivors fear further discrimination (job loss, more physical assaults, family disowning them, teens vandalizing their homes) from outing themselves, or they fear that their local police department just won't care. Even more sadly, many victims eventually see those fears justified. In some cases, the victims weren't even gay, but the perpetrator saw them as gay and attacked them for it; all of that stigma I just mentioned can still haunt the victims and keep them from taking action.

Douglas Victor Janoff, a policy advisor for the Government of Canada, examines many of the same problems I mention above. While conducting extensive research for his book *Pink Blood: Homophobic Violence in Canada*, Janoff found hundreds of cases between 1990 and 2005 where people suffered attacks because of their perceived sexual orientation. Repeatedly, the media, the courts, the police, and sometimes even health-care providers treated the victims as criminals or as deserving what happened to them. Even brutal murders often led to a mild sentence, if any at all. Despite the frequency and savagery of these crimes, Janoff saw that no national statistic-gatherings or policies existed within Canada's government or police departments to deter or keep track of anti-gay hate crimes. Trials often involved vague, overlapping, and contradictory terms like "homosexual panic" or "homosexual advances," which demonized the victim and provoked sympathy for the assailant.

Janoff avoids pessimism, however. Instead, he invites his readers to learn from past and current failures to prevent homophobic assaults. His book shows legal options that can help victims and activists expose and stop anti-gay violence. It also acknowledges and encourages the trends among certain police departments to reach out to the gay community in efforts to make Canada a safer place.

Will you help make America a safer place? You might say that you won't support bills or policies that would counter discrimination or violence against gays, because you fear that others will see you as "validating the homosexual lifestyle." Gays will exist, whether you "validate" us or not; we aren't parking permits. The question here isn't whether you approve of homosexuality but whether you approve of discrimination and violence. By refusing to work against discrimination and violence, and by blocking the efforts of others to do so, you give tacit approval to discrimination and violence.

Those problems would still exist if you worked against them. However, at least you can show them as wrong, and you can give the legal system the power to punish those crimes—not to punish thoughts, but to punish actual acts of harassment, assault, etc. Surely you see that as a fair and just cause. A safer country benefits all people who live in that country, even the "normal guys."

# "I'M NOT QUEER, SO WHY I SHOULD CARE ABOUT THOSE PEOPLE OR GAY RIGHTS?"

Because "those people" belong to your community, and belong to the same environment that you and I help create. Do you want an environment of discrimination, injustice, and violence? Do you want an environment where you might lose your rights or your life at any moment, because someone decided you belong to the wrong group?

Aside from the fact that hate crimes against gays sometimes target nongays that someone mistook as gay, please keep in mind that prejudices often overlap. In his book *Homophobia: A History*, Byrne Fone convincingly establishes the fact that prejudices on the basis of religion, gender, race, and class share a long historical thread with homophobia; for example, he proves how the hatred of feminine men actually grows from the view of women as somehow inferior to men.

Warren J. Blumenfeld edited and contributed to a must-read anthology, *Homophobia: How We All Pay the Price*. In the essays that book contains, he and his fellow contributors show a variety of ways that homophobia hurts nongays. A tiny sampling of those ways follows: children who seek out sexual encounters to prove their heterosexuality, boys who think they must act violently and hide their compassion, girls who suppress their sports interests or even their career interests because someone might call them lesbians. Blumenfeld ends the collection by giving examples of how to conduct workshops that help people see how homophobia affects them and how to reduce it.

As far as gay rights go, I like the term "gay equality," because gays want equal rights—not special rights, and not special discrimination. All Americans need equality, if we want to truly live up to the ideals of the Constitution. Therefore, all Americans should care about gay equality. The obvious fact that the majority outnumbers the minority should not give the majority the right to discriminate against the minority, as we continue to learn with regard to race and religion.

In *How To Make The World A Better Place For Gays And Lesbians*, Una Fahy says that the end of homophobia would help society in general, by reducing tension, and by destroying the need for men to prove their masculinity through acts of violence and aggression. She further argues that heterosexuals need to encourage gays and lesbians to come out, because destroying homophobia and the closet would lead to more honest and productive lives for everyone.

Progress will require a lot more gays and their supporters working to disseminate truthful information in an atmosphere that sees the act of telling anti-gay lies as "godly" and "taking a stand" but the act of telling the truth about gays as "anti-family" and "promoting the homosexual agenda." I see nothing "godly" or "pro-family" about lying. People base their opinions on what they know, but much of what they know about gays comes from lies, so we must keep exposing the lies. We can use letters to the editor, calls to radio talk shows, papers or speeches in classes, and simple conversations with the people around us.

Please, help make your world a better place for all the people in it. You'll be doing yourself a favor. You should care, because it's your world, and "those people" are your neighbors...maybe even your relatives! You probably don't want your rights denied, so why would you want that to happen to others around you?

# "WE SHOULDN'T HAVE TO SEE GAYS WHEN WE WATCH TV OR MOVIES."

It seems odd that people will love a movie or TV show containing murder, adultery, profanity, deceit, racial slurs, misogyny, thievery, decapitations, etc., but cry "immorality" or "agenda" if it includes a positive representation of a gay character. Do TV detective shows promote murder? Since most cultures condemn murder, should we cry "immorality" over those programs? Of course, those programs depict murder as bad, but what about when TV stations show Westerns? Besides promoting racist misinformation against Native Americans, countless Westerns glorify murder, revenge, prostitution, and drunkenness, so why not cry "agenda"?

I also find it odd that, if an actor plays gay, many people label that person gay and anti-family, but they never confuse the same actor with her/his roles as vampire, surgeon, astronaut, etc., and they never label the same actor anti-family for playing a wife-beater, adulterer, etc.

When many people see gay TV characters, they complain about TV focusing too much on sexuality, but they won't say the same when they see a show about heterosexuals. Even the most wholesome family shows deal with puberty, crushes, love, marriage, and reproduction; in other words, they deal with sexuality.

Even nature documentaries contain sexual themes. Unless a show limits its characters to an asexual monk living alone in the Arctic, it cannot avoid sexuality. Then again, he might encounter the Arctic wolf, a species that relies on a bisexual social structure.

Gay people exist, and, as such, will appear within the arts. Despite our smaller number, we seem to flood all the arts, so why should we not express ourselves in our work, and why should we not use our talents to counter the false representations we see of ourselves? If you saw yourself misrepresented and then found a chance to challenge the falsehood, wouldn't you take it?

In the mid-1990s, PFLAG (Parents, Families, and Friends of Lesbians and Gays) created TV commercials that each dealt with one of two topics: the high number of gay teen suicides or the high rate of anti-gay violence. Disguising censorship with the usual "anti-family" rhetoric, most stations refused to carry those much-needed TV spots, leaving gay teens to simply die. Following the logic of those stations, should we see it as "anti-family" to expose and discourage hate crimes and teen suicide but "pro-family" to air programming like tabloid news programs, reality television, trashy talk shows, and slasher movies? Such hostility toward gay-friendly public service announcements continues, even in the 21$^{st}$ century!

# "I WOULD ACCEPT GAYS, BUT I BELIEVE IN FAMILY VALUES."

Gays belong to families, with parents, siblings, and relatives. Many gays have children, either because they discovered or dealt with their orientation after or during a heterosexual relationship, or because they used adoption or some other method. Gays also create families by simply fostering their friendships with other members of the gay community and with nongays who believe in unconditional love. Often, the parent of a gay person will achieve hero status in the gay community by also serving as a parent to gays whose real parents reject them.

I cannot take the term "family values" seriously when it calls for families to reject their own children, often driving them to homelessness or suicide. I cannot take it seriously when it causes gay people to hate themselves. I cannot take it seriously when it causes parents to put children into programs that confuse and hurt them, leaving them with the feeling that they must pretend to be someone else in order for their mother and father to accept them. I cannot take it seriously when it amounts to nothing but hate-promoting legalism.

To me, family values means valuing one's family, not telling them, "Be heterosexual, or be disowned." When a value system drives someone's children to isolation, abandonment, depression, and suicide, it obviously needs repair.

Often, the gay child in an otherwise nongay family will end up caring for an invalid parent, because the other siblings now must take care of their own children. However, the gay child will less likely appear in the parent's will and often had been disowned by the parent until the parent's time of need. While providing special care, that child must endure the parent's homophobic taunts, and her/his lover must endure even crueler treatment. These sacrifices on the part of gays go unnoticed by society and the media. I call such sacrifices family values—valuing our families, even if they mistreat us.

# "Family members spending time with their gay relatives would suggest that they endorse that lifestyle."

Disowning, pushing away, or avoiding your gay relatives won't turn them into heterosexuals. It will probably hurt them. It might make them resent you and your value system. It might make them lonely or even suicidal on holidays, especially in the case of gay teens. It might make them a lot of things, but it won't make them heterosexual. Such approaches don't work for making a relative stop loving a member of another race, so what makes you think they will work for making a relative stop loving within the same gender?

You won't live on this world for all that long. Why not spend some of that precious time with your gay relatives? Instead of avoiding them, why not make them a part of your life? Even if you would rather not admit it, you probably have relatives who lie, gossip, get drunk, have pre-marital sex, hold grudges, or treat people unfairly. Are you condoning all of that by spending time with those relatives or inviting them to family gatherings? No. You're just acknowledging them as a part of your family.

How much time do you think you have left? How much time do you think they have left? You wouldn't be endorsing anything by letting them share your life with you, and you're not accomplishing anything by treating them like lepers.

You're family, and they need you. Don't let them down.

# "THEY LIVE THAT GAY LIFESTYLE."

Statements about the "gay lifestyle" often rely on a refusal to see all human beings (gay or otherwise) as complex, intelligent, and unique. How often will individuals or the media refer to the left-handed lifestyle, Methodist lifestyle, Arizona lifestyle, blue-eyed lifestyle, Hispanic lifestyle, or heterosexual lifestyle? As human beings, gay people live individual lives, not a lifestyle. If nongays must group us into the concept of "lifestyle," they should at least use the plural "lifestyles."

Far from fitting into a single lifestyle, LGBTs epitomize human diversity: the gay male lumberjack, the fierce drag queen by night who wears a uniform and pumps gas during the day, the quiet librarian who thinks "going out" means grocery shopping, the teacher in her forties who keeps winning awards for excellence from people who would fire her if they knew why she never married, the lady cop no one wants to cross but everyone seems to love, the nelly college boy with the sharp wit, the strong-willed woman who won't let her wheelchair become all that she is, the retired female couple celebrating their thirtieth anniversary, the biker whose stomach now hangs a little too much for that leather vest, the members of Log Cabin Republicans, the workers at an AIDS hospice who now find themselves caring largely for heterosexuals who saw AIDS as a "gay disease," and that one enduringly eligible bachelor in the local bridge club.

I am none of those people. I am only me. I am not a lifestyle. I don't live, have, pursue, or want a lifestyle. Being gay doesn't obligate me to beg for anyone's acceptance by pretending to support causes that I don't really support. It also doesn't obligate me to wear $60 T-shirts with the name of some snooty fashion designer.

Many gays will use the terms "gay lifestyle" or "alternative lifestyle," even if they don't see gayness as a choice. I despise those terms, but they're certainly better than a lot of the other terms that people use for gays. Many gays hate the term "gay lifestyle," while some use it to refer to living openly gay—i.e., as another way of saying "being out." On a scarier note, though, many gays will even try to convince each other that we can only earn the right to be ourselves if we all learn to think, believe, act, talk, and dress exactly alike; views differ on how to properly carry out all of that molding into a "lifestyle," but it sounds both scary and boring to me.

Of course, I keep using the term "many gays" in place of "gays" because we are not some collective mind, as I keep pointing out. Our views conflict with each other, just as the views of heterosexuals conflict with each other. We do not all hold the same views, values, or beliefs. We live lives. Lives.

# "IT'S AN INSULT TO AFRICAN AMERICANS TO COMPARE BEING GAY TO BEING BLACK."

That statement is an insult. Imagine if someone said, "It's an insult to Native Americans to compare being black to being Indian." That would sound like the person saw blacks as inferior to Native Americans, just as the statement above characterizes gays as inferior to blacks.

People use comparisons to make points, to help explain, and even to look for solutions. If I compare two problems in two different states then discuss the different ways those states handle them, I am not calling both states or both problems the same. Rather, I am observing common ground and possible common solutions, learning from similarities and differences. Gays can learn much from African Americans because—like it or not—gay history overlaps with black history.

Many of the people who harass gays now were too busy harassing African Americans or worrying about Communism to notice us before. The Southern Baptist Convention, for example, waited until the late twentieth century to start making amends for its long heritage of racism, and it now spends much of its time finding ways to punish anyone who tries to grant gays the equal rights the Constitution should give us—and even to distort the Constitution into a way of blocking our rights. However, my comments here relate mostly to the convention itself, not to all the members of Southern Baptist churches. Many Southern Baptists take offense at the news from the SBC's often divided and often divisive meetings; some Southern Baptists belong to a group called "Honesty," which tries to overcome anti-gay attitudes in its denomination. Also, countless Southern Baptists give to mission funds that help needy people all over the world; any criticisms I give of the SBC refer to weaknesses in an otherwise benevolent institution.

Turning to groups without such redeeming qualities, the KKK and other white power organizations seem increasingly pre-occupied with gays. The more we work for equality and visibility, the more they try to scare us back into the dark recesses of the closet. Not surprisingly, numerous otherwise fair-minded people turn a blind eye to those activities, just as they turned a blind eye to these groups before (and sometimes even during) the civil rights movement. Like African Americans, gays face people who think patriotism or out-of-context Bible verses can justify a denial of our basic human rights, including the right to live.

Of course, most blacks cannot hide their skin color in order to gain acceptance, though many used to try—and some still do. I would no more call gay the same as black than I would call black the same as Hispanic, Native American, Asian, left-handed, disabled, Jewish, Islamic, or any other difference. Only a gay person can fully understand the gay experience; only a black person can fully understand the black experience. The same goes for those other groups I just listed.

Still, the fact that gays live outside the majority, often facing mistreatment by that majority, gives us a certain kinship with people of color, including blacks. Our kinship also comes from the fact that many gay people also happen to be African American, and from the less fortunate fact that both groups suffer from an unusually high mortality rate among its young men—blacks because of factors that include AIDS and homicide, gays because of factors that include AIDS and teen suicide.

Furthermore, America's gay equality movement became increasingly visible shortly after the civil rights movement gained momentum during the 1960s, and it still relies heavily on the tactics and teachings of civil rights leaders, particularly the Rev. Dr. Martin Luther King, Jr. In fact, King's widow later became a frequent advocate of gay equality. Blacks made faster and larger strides than openly gay people, possibly because most blacks could not retreat to anything like the closet.

Certain blacks make extremely racist, homophobic, or anti-Semitic comments, in between their complaints about bigotry against blacks. As with certain people in all groups—including gays—those individuals only object to discrimination when it targets their group. We all need to address bigotry, and admit that it creeps into everyone's minds. Instead of trying to pretend it out of existence, we should fight the hatred that exists within others and ourselves.

Some African Americans say that "an oppressed people can't discriminate." Actually, I think all people can, and all people do. Bitterness over past injustice only exacerbates the problem. We all fail to learn from the discrimination or injustice we face; instead, we turn around and mistreat someone else for not looking, acting, or thinking exactly like ourselves.

Everyone suffers from the natural human fault of bigotry; no one escapes it forever. The gay community, the black community, the Christian community, and every other community suffers from bigotry, because human beings comprise all those communities. All those communities must fight bigotry. They can start by realizing that those communities overlap and intersect in both good and bad ways. We need each other much more than we might want to admit. All the gays who discriminate against blacks and other groups show hypocrisy by protesting bigotry while practicing it; however, that works both ways.

If you're (1) black and (2) racist, anti-Semitic, or homophobic, please think about the fact that your bigotry helps keep the crosses burning. All of it hurts all of us, and our support of it encourages people in other groups to hate our group. I know we can't completely eradicate bigotry, but we can keep working against it, instead of simply redirecting it.

When we fight it, we help ourselves and each other. When we redirect it, it might circle back around to us.

# "THE PARTS DON'T FIT."

You obviously lack imagination.

It might make many people uncomfortable to think that heterosexuals engage in any sexual activity other than penis-to-vagina penetration. Try reading some nongay sexual publications; whether erotic or clinical, they contain many variations from that theme. A man and a woman trying to please each other might not always limit themselves to the one most obvious act.

Anyway, why only focus on sex? The love between two consenting adults in a romantic relationship matters much more than how well their parts fit together. Many couples, gay and nongay, reduce or even give up sex at some point in their relationship, even if they still love each other. Certain disabilities or health problems prevent some loving couples from engaging in sex, but not from loving each other. And some loving couples simply choose a nonsexual relationship from the beginning, which may or may not change at a later time.

Couples express their love, and even find their love, in many ways that don't involve their genitals. They like companionship, sharing their lives with someone who will listen to them or even enjoy quiet moments with them. I'm talking about gay and nongay couples here.

Why can't you think of love when you think of gays? Yes, we can love each other, even if you can't love us. Love fits.

# "IF WE WEREN'T SO TOLERANT OF GAYS, THERE WOULDN'T BE ANY."

No law or taboo can stop gays from existing, from being born. Gays probably exist in the same number everywhere, from countries where we receive the death penalty, to countries where we enjoy equal rights with our fellow human beings, to America—the country where we find ourselves torn between our patriotism and those who want American freedoms to only apply to themselves.

When Boris Yeltsin lifted the death penalty for gays in Russia, it turned out that a huge gay underground had long existed there. The Germany of the late nineteenth century was largely tolerant of gays and Jews; as Germany moved toward intolerance, it also moved toward violence and oppression. Germany has now moved back toward tolerance, and the German authorities work against the activities of the many hate groups that seem entrenched there. Mexico, Cuba, and India hardly treat gays fairly, so why do gays keep showing up in those environments?

We have seen how fear of many groups leads to injustice of all sorts, from internment to genocide. It still happens all over the world, for all sorts of absurd reasons that always go back to fear and hatred of the dreaded "other."

In America, intolerance against gays creates an atmosphere of hatred and self-hatred, leading to addictions, suicides (especially teen suicides), hate crimes, evictions, job discrimination, and disowned children. Tolerance helps prevent those problems. Any responsible citizens should at least consider tolerance and education as possible solutions to such dilemmas, even if they find homosexuality objectionable.

Christian fundamentalists in particular should remember Matthew 25, where Jesus teaches that failing to help the poor, the sick, the imprisoned, and the mistreated amounts to a rejection of God. What about PWA's (People With AIDS), victims of hate crimes, gays disowned by their parents, or gays who lost their job over their orientation? Don't your values call you to help those people?

# "I WOULDN'T MIND GAYS IF IT WEREN'T FOR THEM CHECKING ME OUT."

This remark seems to mostly come from and refer to males. I've never heard a woman make the remark about lesbians, but women and girls often complain about heterosexual males eyeing them like a piece of meat. Becoming the object of unwanted gawking and passes might help heterosexual men empathize with women and stop treating them like the prize behind door number one. From the bragging of all too many nongay men, women often sound more like a vagina than an entire human being. No wonder some nongay women prefer the company of gay men.

I can't think of how many times I've heard so-called "real men" boasting about "going out to get some." Men in general can seem overly sexually aggressive, but many women lack the strength, stature, and social advantages that most men could use for fighting off sexual assault. Therefore, I see unwanted sexual advances made toward women as more threatening than those made toward men but all sexual harassment as inappropriate and unacceptable.

Just say "Quit staring at me" or something to that effect. If needed, say "I'm not interested" or "I'm not gay." If those steps fail, talk to the owner or manager of the place where the advances occur. Some gays will inwardly appreciate your getting rid of the nuisance who made them (and other gays) look so bad, just as you sometimes like to see certain heterosexual males get tossed out or turned down after you tire of hearing their bragging and their pathetic lines.

Still, a confidant, mature man will only use threats of violence as an absolute last resort. Just as you sometimes mistake the friendliness or concern of a woman as sexual interest, your gay suitor might also suffer from a case of wishful thinking. Take it as flattery, but defuse it in a manner that shows you aren't some insecure little man who must prove his heterosexuality through violence. By the way, if certain women flirt with you, that doesn't mean all women want you; the same goes for if certain gay men flirt with you.

# "HAVING GAY PARENTS MAKES CHILDREN GAY."

According to the American Psychological Association, children of gays are no more likely to be gay than children of nongays. The APA also contradicts the lies that group gays with child molesters. Male heterosexuals commit most rapes and child molestation. Furthermore, the APA tells us that gays are no more likely than nongays to abuse children or to have been abused as children.

Out of the countless gays I've met, only a few said they were abused as children. I've also met some heterosexuals who had been abused as children, but it didn't make them gay. Yes, abuse happens within both groups, but that doesn't mean the abuse caused or changed their sexual orientation.

Many parents will abuse or disown their children for being gay, but that is an effect of homophobia, not a cause of homosexuality. In some cases, the parents of gays aren't homophobic, but those children still fear possible homophobia and thus distance themselves from their parents. The problem is homophobia, not homosexuality.

Gay parents are no more or less likely than heterosexual parents to raise gay children. Besides, heterosexuals produce both gay and heterosexual children, so what makes people think gay parents only produce gay children? Parents don't make their children gay or heterosexual, and being gay isn't something that people "do" to their parents or their children.

If anything, children in gay homes, like children in interracial homes, will grow up with a stronger awareness of society's need for tolerance and compassion. These children will more likely help America build a less violent society, instead of finding excuses to hurt and kill the people they meet. In fact, people in or from interracial marriages would make good allies for gays, because they know about the ways many people use scripture and tradition to promote bigotry.

# "GAY PEOPLE SHOULD TRY TO BE CURED."

Prayer, Bible study, electro-shock, hormonal therapy, physical therapy, radiation therapy, lobotomy, insane asylums, anaphrodisiacs, exorcism, torture, heterosexual marriage, masturbation to heterosexual pornography, and gender-stereotype programming all fail to change one's natural orientation. Groups in the ex-gay movement lure gays into an expensive and dangerous scam that claims to serve that purpose but only leads to self-hatred. These sexist groups dwell on men and masculinity, while ignoring or belittling women. They show their fear of women when they rely on the out-dated Freudian claim that homosexuality results from a domineering mother and an absent or abusive father. In other cases, they will even convince gays to avoid their same-gender parents, under the argument that one's same-gender parent can somehow make one gay; so much for family values.

We can cure hatred and self-hatred, but we can't cure sexual orientation. And, please, conditioning a man to get an erection in a woman's presence proves that conditioning works, but not that the ex-gay movement works; conditioning could also cause a man to get an erection when he sees chocolate. Most women can fake an orgasm, and most gay men can arouse themselves for a woman by simply fantasizing about a man.

Leigh W. Rutledge's usually light-hearted book *The New Gay Book of Lists* takes a sickening twist when he describes several of the cures through the ages and warns against the possible forced gene therapy that might come with the common acceptance of gay gene theories. Many gays and their supporters see gay gene evidence as promising, because it proves both that gayness is not a choice and that gays deserve treatment as a separate minority group. Others within the gay community note that it might forge an unlikely alliance between gays and religious fundamentalists, as some anti-abortion activists might suddenly support abortion if they thought the fetus might grow into a gay person. Whether we see it as genetic or not, we don't need anyone to save us from homosexuality; if anything, we need saving from the people who want to hurt us or turn us into clones of themselves.

The ex-gay movement claims it saves people from AIDS, but it will encourage gays to break off long-term relationships and will even resort to the lie that no gays engage in long-term relationships. The newly unattached gay will then feel the same longings but will express them only outside a committed relationship, and will not buy protection in advance. Ex-gays also gloss over the fact that lesbians are at much lower risk for AIDS than heterosexual women, so saving women from AIDS would require converting them to—not from—lesbianism.

Of course, re-closeted cases will act cured if it means their families will accept them again. The ex-gay movement either fails to see or pretends not to see the difference between two concepts: (1) the fact of going back into the closet, (2) the fiction of changing one's sexual orientation.

Many parents feign unconditional love, telling their children, "You can talk to us about anything." But if one of the children calls their bluff by coming out to them, that child might become homeless and parent-less. In many cases, the child will commit suicide, unable to live without the respect and love of family. With such conditions, some of America's least scrupulous preachers and Christian psychologists know they can tap into a lot of wallets and purses, just by saying, "Come to us, and God will cure you of homosexuality."

No reputable long-term research suggests that these cures work, so the leaders of the ex-gay movement will eventually tell their victims they should either enter a heterosexual marriage anyway, or simply remain abstinent. Would those groups force heterosexuals to remain abstinent, except when making babies? In fact, considering the modern problem of overpopulation, they could limit all heterosexuals to baby-making quotas. Of course those propositions sound insane and unconstitutional, so why impose the same insanity and unconstitutionality on gays? How dare these groups give a human being a life sentence of loneliness, just for being different?

Most of all, these groups teach gays to resent themselves. Gays can suppress their orientation for long periods, but it will always resurface. After each resurfacing of same-gender longing, the ex-gay movement will then cause its victims to see themselves as continual failures, driving them closer to suicide.

I see the ex-gay movement as a failure. Their lists of "cured gays" includes bisexuals, as well as heterosexuals who had merely experimented with same-gender sex, and even gays who abandoned the pointless ex-gay movement and returned to honestly living out their orientation. The ex-gay movement only contributes to the self-hatred that leads gays to addiction, depression, and suicide.

If being different in some way makes Susie unhappy, what should we see as the real problem: her difference, or the bigotry of others? If Susie managed to "correct" her difference, wouldn't she just endorse bigotry by shaping her life to accommodate it? Won't the bigots just find some other excuse for rejecting her or some other group that they elect as "wrong" or "abnormal"? Should she want the approval of hateful people, or should she look for happiness by being herself and by finding others who both accept and admire her differences?

What makes so many people think that uniformity begets happiness, or that happiness requires uniformity? I can be happy without being like you, just as you can be happy without being like me.

Our goal should change from curing individuality to curing the fear of individuality. We need to quit punishing the victims, and start helping people free themselves from the negative feelings that others try to impose on them. Working together, we can learn to accept ourselves and each other.

In his book *Anything but Straight: Unmasking the Scandals and Lies Behind the Ex-Gay Myth*, Wayne R. Besen reveals not only his extensive research on the ex-gay movement but also his experiences gleaned from going undercover in their meetings. He also provides extensive resources. I highly recommend that book, or at least looking at what the American Psychological Association says about the subject online (http://apa.org).

# "HOMOSEXUALITY IS A MENTAL ILLNESS."

In their pamphlet *Answers to Your Questions About Sexual Orientation and Homosexuality*, the American Psychological Association (APA) states that this misconception stemmed from the fact that "most studies only involved lesbians and gay men in therapy." The Religious Right often claims that the APA changed their position because of pressure from gay groups or because of a lack of new research, but the APA clearly states something different.

Explaining that less-biased research led them to quit referring to homosexuality in the traditional terminology of "disorder" or "illness," the APA warns against attempts to cure sexual orientation. Just as the church once threatened to execute people for saying the Earth revolves around the sun, the Religious Right wants to stop the release of knowledge that can prove gay people simply exist: not as a choice, phase, fad, curse, philosophy, movement, sickness, or something we "outgrow." We simply exist. Unfortunately, the APA fails to speak out when parents institutionalize their gay children under the guise of "gender identity disorder" (GID).

From my experiences and the findings of researchers, I would say a lot of extreme or obsessive homophobia results from certain gays refusing to accept and integrate their sexual orientation. I've known many closet cases that went around making homophobic remarks, before or after coming out to me. Sadly, I used to take part in such remarks, hoping for acceptance, hoping to destroy a part of myself by hating it in someone else; such desperate measures can only hurt the individual and society. According to many psychologists, extreme or obsessive homophobia usually masks one's own unwanted sexual orientation, or insecurity over something else that might make them feel different from the norm. People often make their secrets obvious by trying a little too hard to hide them under argument and accusation.

If you seem obsessively homophobic, it makes me wonder if you're secretly a gay person who just can't deal with it. Psychologists call your tendency "projection." When you can't accept a part of yourself, you project that part onto others and criticize it in them, or you even physically assault them for the trait you share. It draws attention from yourself, possibly even winning you the admiration of other insecure people. Counseling can help you accept yourself and others. On the other hand, if you say, "I'm not gay, but I'm comfortable around gays," I'll find your self-confidence and maturity impressive, even if you disapprove of homosexuality.

# "IF EVERYONE WERE GAY, WE'D STOP HAVING CHILDREN, AND DIE OUT."

Should we hate celibate or sterile people for not having children? Will nuns cause us to die out? Should we tell heterosexuals they can't marry unless they plan to propagate? Should we encourage violent people to propagate, thus putting children in a violent home?

If human life involves nothing more than birth, reproduction, and death, how can we consider ourselves a higher life-form than insects? I can live a meaningful life and make important contributions without ever fathering a child.

Those who reproduce over-compensate for those who don't reproduce; for overwhelming evidence of that fact, visit an orphanage, homeless shelter, unemployment line, or third-world country. For even more evidence, look at all the grandparents raising their grandchildren and all the children having children. We aren't even close to "dying out."

Consider the consistently small percentage of gays in each area, and that many of them enter heterosexual marriages, to protect themselves from discrimination. Also consider the fact that science now offers asexual reproduction, so we can make babies without taking part in heterosexual intercourse. Gays can even make babies the old-fashioned way, with someone who agrees to serve as a surrogate parent.

That "dying out" warning suggests a person's life only matters in as much as that person can create more people. I say that a person's life simply matters, with or without creating more people. Enriching the lives of ourselves and others can make our life more wonderful, but that enrichment can come in ways other than reproduction.

You might tell your son that he needs to father children so he can carry on the family name. What a terrible reason for bringing a human being into the world! Won't he wonder if that's the only reason you wanted him? His ancestors will still have existed, no matter what he does or doesn't do. What if your last name is Smith? What if your son wants to carry on the family name through adoption? What if he wants to change his last name?

Most women still relinquish their last names when they marry. Since those women can't carry on their family names, do women have less value than men? Many people think so, but I don't.

Gays have plenty of horny heterosexual relatives who go around carrying on the family name with reckless abandon. At this second, countless people are having sex. Many of those sexual unions will cause conception, intentionally or unintentionally. While good parenting requires a great deal of acumen, making a baby doesn't. So why place so much emphasis on making babies?

Maybe nature intended gays as natural population control—something we need in a world of depleted resources, overcrowded streets, overcrowded jails, overcrowded schools, homeless families, overflowing landfills, overflowing sewage, malnourished communities, chemically polluted water supplies, fast-spreading viruses, over-used soil, endangered animals, and shrinking forests. If that sounds implausible, explain the frequent homosexuality within the animal kingdom, and please resist the temptation of saying dolphins choose to be gay.

Most animal species know instinctively that overpopulation lowers the quality of life for everyone; the few species that reproduce in extraordinary numbers mostly do so to compensate for a short life span or a high mortality rate. By breeding like rabbits, human beings exhaust the supplies their children and grandchildren will need—even the most basic supplies that we generally take for granted, including drinkable water.

By over-breeding, the human race destroys its only habitat: the Earth. Religious fundamentalists in particular should find that assault disturbing, considering that the Bible says God created this planet, and that God commanded humanity to serve as Creation's stewards. How dare we destroy God's Creation? Yes, God said "be fruitful and multiply, and replenish the earth" during the creation, but He said it specifically as a command to Adam and Eve, who were supposedly the only two people on Earth (Genesis 1:28). I doubt God would make that same command to all six billion (and growing) of the people on Earth today, especially considering how many of that number live in poverty and malnutrition. Humanity's attempts at fruitfulness have succeeded too well for too long; we'll eventually multiply beyond what the Earth can hold.

Today, fruitful parenting requires a lot less multiplying and a lot more nurturing. We need to take better care of the children who already exist, instead of constantly rushing to produce millions more. We need to quit treating children like the results of some failed laboratory experiment. Instead of trying to improve and guide their existing children, too many parents start the experiment over by making more and more children. We need to stress pre-natal care, education, drug-prevention programs, job skills, and other measures that will help our children, but we certainly don't need to pressure every human being into mindless, ceaseless breeding.

Despite our social nature, human beings require a lot of space, a lot of what people used to call "elbow room." It relieves tension. By overpopulating, we constantly press against each other, escalating the tensions and violence that space could reduce; we even turn animals against us by invading and shrinking their habitats. Some might look at this argument and falsely claim that I'm trying to convince everyone to become gay. Actually, I just mean that most cultures put way too much emphasis on reproduction and way too little emphasis on valuing the people already on Earth.

Everyone (gay and nongay) needs to behave sexually responsibly—either by not having sex, by sticking with one partner for life, or by practicing safer sex. Condoms only fail to work as well as intended because we fail to use them properly…if at all. Sexual responsibility throughout society would stop most STD's and most unwanted pregnancies, but it wouldn't cause humanity to die out; gays won't cause that either.

# "YOU DESERVE WHAT HAPPENS TO YOU, BECAUSE YOU CHOOSE TO BE GAY."

Differences from the norm can't justify discrimination and violence. If I chose to join a Baptist church in the mostly Mormon Salt Lake City, would that justify someone robbing me of my home, job, or life? Your argument not only tramples on the Constitution of the United States of America but also relies on a false assumption. Contrary to the views of those who could not possibly know what I feel or choose, I disagree with the idea of my gayness as a so-called "choice" or "lifestyle choice." I can't speak for other gay people, because I can't look inside their minds, but I know that I did not choose to be gay.

Many people falsely claim that all gays refer to our gayness as an "alternative lifestyle" or "lifestyle choice," which supposedly justifies any atrocity committed against us. Some gays use those terms, but most (not all) gays will say they never chose their gayness. Bisexuals may have more choice in the matter, but I am not bisexual. I am 100% gay. I could choose denial, the closet, coming out completely, only coming out to certain people, living the lie of a fake marriage, or many other options. Regardless of which options I chose, I would remain gay.

Why choose to become a target for hatred, discrimination, blame, threats, and violence? Why choose something that often leads to the loss of parental love and support? Take for example a young man in Texas who believed he could tell his parents anything. One day, he came out to them; contrary to his belief, they disowned him. He shot himself, leaving a note that said he couldn't live without love. That happens all the time, all over the world. In fact, gay teens are much more likely than other teens to attempt suicide. Do you even care? If gayness were always a choice, wouldn't those teens just solve the problem by choosing not to be gay anymore? Many gay teens evade the problem by pretending not to be gay, and some that regret coming out will evade the problem by falsely claiming God cured their gayness, but they remain gay. Only a gay person can fully imagine the pain those young people experience, but I doubt most people would choose that pain.

Should we hate all black people because of the unusually high crime rate among some African American neighborhoods? No. Should we hate all Middle Eastern people because some of them are anti-American terrorists? No. Should we hate all people from Japan and Germany because of World War II or all people from Communist countries because of our various battles with Communist governments? No. Should we hate all people from a country whose founders allowed the slaughter of native peoples, the slavery of blacks, and the near slavery of women and poor people? Oops! That's America. But the answer is still no.

We shouldn't hate anyone.

If it were a choice, it would still be my choice, and it would not justify discrimination and violence against me. And if it were a choice, I would have chosen heterosexuality when I was younger, saving myself the difficult journey of coming to terms with my sexual orientation, my internalized homophobia, and my fears of rejection and hatred. But I'm happy, now that I have accepted my orientation. If it were a choice now, I would choose to be who I am, including gay. Changing my orientation would be no less devastating to me now than being kicked out of my beloved America; it is that deeply interwoven into the aspects of myself that I most cherish. I like myself, and I really don't need you to like me.

I'm not saying I've given up on changing or becoming a better person; I still work constantly at both, but I'm changing and becoming a better person who just happens to be gay. When people get upset at gay-friendly groups for supposedly "losing hope" in our ability to change, they miss the point: there's nothing wrong with being gay. My hope is that all people can live honestly with themselves and peacefully with each other. I haven't given up hope in myself or in humanity; I've just quit thinking that God meant for everyone to be heterosexual, just like He didn't mean for all people to have white skin, blonde hair, and blue eyes.

I choose to live a happy and productive life, with or without your approval. You can call that my choice.

# "ACCEPTING HOMOSEXUALITY DESTROYED EMPIRES LIKE GREECE AND ROME, AND EVEN LED TO THE HOLOCAUST."

Empires conquered each other constantly in the ancient world. Their fall had nothing to do with homosexuality, but much to do with wars, infighting, politics, and even environmental problems like lead poisoning. Blaming gays requires a blatant rewrite of history and reality.

But the distortion of history doesn't stop there. Some Web sites, books, and pamphlets falsely identify the World War II Nazi Party as a mostly gay organization. Almost all historians will disagree with those claims, just as they disagree with the common Aryan claims that the Holocaust never happened to gays, that it never happened to Jews, or that the Jews themselves caused the Holocaust. Many people will question the misinformation when it refers to Jews, but will become blissfully gullible when the lies condemn gays.

The United States Holocaust Memorial Museum in Washington features exhibits and records that prove thousands of gays died in the Holocaust. For the Nazis, the pink triangle on gay men served the same purpose as the Star of David on Jews. In fact, the Nazi doctors and scientists singled out gays for some of their cruelest experiments and tortures, while the Nazi party also relegated gay men to some of the most grueling and hazardous hard labor.

Lesbians usually became the victims of forced marriages, or just forced sex. Though lesbians apparently went into the concentration camps in smaller numbers than gay men, the ones there received a black triangle, a sign of deviance. Today, both gays and lesbians generally use the pink triangle in reference to the camps, as most people more readily identify the color pink with homosexuality.

The next time you see someone with a pink triangle, please think about the fact that it means for gays to remember the past and push on for equality. The person wearing it is probably gay, or the friend or family member of a gay person.

We know from Hitler's speeches that the Nazis saw themselves as protecting their country, and as stopping certain groups from destroying the supposedly righteous majority. Such hateful attitudes can easily rise again, any place in the world, leading to discrimination and violence. It happens again and again. We need to see pink triangles, black triangles, Stars of David, and all the other symbols that can help us remember the ugly truth about the Holocaust; and we desperately need more education about the Holocaust, to stop history from repeating itself in other countries, or even here in America.

# "THEY RECRUIT."

Every time I hear this one, I think of the closing scene from the famous coming-out episode of the cancelled-but-classic TV sitcom *Ellen*. As a reward for the "recruitment" of Ellen, singer Melissa Etheridge gives Laura Dern a toaster oven! That silly image resonates with countless gays because most of us hear that silly "They recruit" line so often.

Read through all the problems I mention in this essay—all the dangers, fears, confusion, and hostilities that gays face. Exactly what sort of recruitment promise would we use: "Be gay and be hated"? It hardly sounds appealing. Gays simply find each other and try to educate each other, but we are already gay before we find each other.

As I pointed out before, some gays are overly aggressive in seeking sex partners. Certain gays (and please notice the word "certain") find nongay sex partners through pressure tactics, but that doesn't change the partner's sexual orientation. No one "becomes" gay. In fact, the partner might resent gays even more after such a forceful seduction, especially if it involves coercion through drugs or alcohol. That isn't recruitment; it's rape. I can't and won't justify that, and I hope the gay individuals who act that way will realize how much they hurt their victims, themselves, and the gay community with their reckless, heartless actions.

Many nongays also pursue sex partners too aggressively, using alcohol, drugs, violence, or threats to get what they want, but no one calls that recruitment. Gays encounter constant recruitment efforts from fundamentalists, ex-gay cults, and various well-meaning but ill-informed relatives. That attempted recruitment comes from heterosexuals, not from gays.

I don't believe people can voluntarily change their sexual orientation, so I don't believe that gays can recruit in the sense of turning people gay. We might convince gays to join a gay organization, to visit a gay bar, to buy a gay book, or to simply come out. In your strained use of homophobic rhetoric, you might see all of that as recruiting people into homosexuality, but those people were already gay. "Coming out" means acknowledging what was already true.

I've even heard or read statements like "The following quote shows gays admit that they recruit." Claims like that one usually introduce something said within a satire. The concept of satire tends to elude people who want to take all words literally, but it involves pretending to take a stand that one actually finds objectionable. Like the famous satires of the Anglican minister Jonathan Swift (*Gulliver's Travels*, etc.), modern satires use sarcastic humor to make important points, while warning against faulty logic, dangerous extremes, etc. For example, Swift's essay

"A Modest Proposal," still often banned by school boards, assails the inhumanity of some governments by seeming to advocate cannibalism.

Many gay writers will feign the stereotypes of gays in order to satirize those stereotypes, but then someone will quote the satire out of context, without clarifying it as satire. In fact, family values groups and writers of letters to the editor rely constantly on such dishonest tactics. They also rely on information and even misinformation about gay fringe groups to represent all gays. Whatever the case, any heterosexual who uses such tactics should prepare to answer the question, "Are you a KKK member?"

Using one quote to represent all gays relies on syllogistic reasoning like the following: "A member of X said/did Y; therefore, all members of X say/do Y." Such reasoning makes as much sense as saying, "I know a teen who likes opera; therefore, all teens like opera." Consider this syllogism: "Most famous black people are athletes, actors, dancers, or musicians. Joe is black. Therefore, Joe can only succeed as an athlete, actor, dancer, or musician." Surely you wouldn't accept that syllogistic reasoning in regard to teens or African Americans, so why accept it in regard to gays?

One gay person saying something is not the same as all gay people saying or thinking that something. Do you agree with every statement made by every heterosexual? Every action taken by every heterosexual? If a heterosexual robs a bank, will you expect headlines that say "Heterosexuals are bank robbers"? Are you heterosexual people, the heterosexual community, "people living the heterosexual lifestyle," or merely an individual human being who happens to be heterosexual? If you agree with that last option, why can't you see gays as individuals? Why see us as all the same person?

We don't recruit, and we don't say we recruit—unless we're mocking that ridiculous notion. There's no recruiting involved in one's sexual orientation.

# "THEY JUST HAVEN'T MET THE RIGHT PERSON OF THE OPPOSITE SEX YET."

It will probably never happen, except as a friend. Gays who marry someone of the opposite sex are usually (a) not yet aware of their sexual orientation, (b) actually bi, or (c) living a lie for family or community standing. In fact, gay men will often marry a friend who must somehow deal with an unplanned pregnancy; it provides the perfect cover for both parties, simply letting everyone see the husband as the father. Lesbians will often marry gay men, though both will replace the marriage bed with covert same-gender relations. Sadly, this dishonesty gives them the acceptance needed for many occupations—in other words, many occupations foster dishonesty.

Even more sadly and dishonestly, many gays will enter into a fake marriage without coming out to their spouse, sincerely hoping that the marriage will change them. Quite often, those gays will eventually start pursuing gay relationships, or just anonymous gay sex, while maintaining their marriage and putting the nongay spouse at risk of STD's.

A fully gay person will only find members of the same gender sexually attractive—and only certain ones of those. Despite all the genetic and hormonal research that suggests innate differences between gays and nongays, no one really understands attraction or tastes. Various scientists tell us the following: a gay man's brain more closely resembles that of a woman than that of a nongay man; the inner ear of gay women often differs from that of nongay women; the fingerprints of gay men are often more like those of women than those of nongay men; the identical twin of a gay person has a 50/50 likelihood of also being gay, even if separated at birth; certain genetic sequences tend to reoccur randomly, possibly including specific genes that cause or influence one's sexual orientation; homosexuality often happens in family clusters, even if the gay relatives never meet; homosexuality occurs constantly within the animal kingdom, often serving social functions (nonviolence, population control, etc.); and hormones secreted during human pregnancies might affect genitalia, body structure, and/or sexual orientation.

Similar findings continue, and I only offered a sampling above. Still, we should keep in mind that (1) some of those studies haven't been reproduced, (2) only certain scientists agree with the concept of gayness as a genetic pre-disposition, (3) no scientists have studied the causes of heterosexuality, and (4) we still know little about tastes or attraction.

Why will a heterosexual woman only find certain men attractive? Why not all of them? Why will a beautiful, intelligent, and ethical woman date a homely, slow-witted, abusive man? Why will two people with nothing in common fall in love? Why will people who may never see each other again fall in love?

Attraction and tastes rarely limit themselves to the boundaries of logic. The same goes for other interests. Why can't I make myself like country music, baseball, or pinto beans?

You might decide that I should marry and have children, just to test your theory that it will "fix" me—that I shouldn't disagree with you until after I've tested your theory in that way. Excuse me, but women and children are human beings, not science experiments. Can you imagine how a heterosexual woman feels when she learns that her husband and the father of her children is gay, how a heterosexual man feels when he learns that his wife and the mother of his children is gay, or how children feel when they learn that one of their parents would rather be with a person of the same sex than with their other parent?

Countless people actually endure that trauma, so they don't have to imagine. You can learn more via groups like Straight Spouse Network or in countless books about spouses who spent years—possibly even decades—trying to make a marriage with a gay person work. I wouldn't wish that struggle on anyone. If you can't be sensitive to the feelings of gays, can't you at least show some compassion towards your fellow heterosexuals?

Maybe you have a heterosexual marriage, one that includes children. Maybe you find that completely rewarding and would never want to lose it. Maybe you depend on it for happiness and a sense of completion. But guess what? Many people (including many heterosexuals) find happiness and a sense of completion without marriage and/or without children. In fact, many people feel that they would have been happier and more complete without their marriage and/or children, or without having children at an early age; such regrets might cause resentment toward their loved ones. Also, some people's jobs, personalities, psychological problems, or whatever else can prevent them from being good parents or good spouses. None of that invalidates your joy in any way. What you have is wonderful, but it isn't for everyone.

To illustrate my point, let me take an example from my life. I take great pleasure in my writing—in the planning, the note taking, the first draft, the revisions, the public readings, and most other aspects of it. The typos, the rejection slips, the lack of media coverage, and many other parts of a writing career can annoy me at times, but I accept the downsides as drawbacks to an otherwise rewarding endeavor. I especially love for others to acknowledge my writing as important or enjoyable. I wouldn't want to live without my writing. However, I understand that many people would never want to become writers. See the metaphor? (Most writers love metaphors!) I don't think everyone should be a writer, just as I don't think that everyone should be a parent, or that everyone should be married to a member of the opposite sex.

As a sort of footnote, though, I have heard from some married gays who came to a place where they were honest about the fact that they couldn't change, and their heterosexual spouse accepted that. Yet, they still decided to stay together. They lived with each other too long to live without each other, even if it meant a sexless marriage. That doesn't mean they would suggest their situation to other couples, but it works for them. I certainly wouldn't condemn that choice, but I condemn the practice of pressuring others into fake marriages.

# "GAYS CAN'T ADOPT, BECAUSE THEIR CHILDREN WILL GET TEASED, AND THAT ISN'T FAIR."

In that case, teach children not to hate. Should we deny parents the right to adopt children of a different race from themselves, for fear that those children will get teased at school? Children will always find excuses to tease, but you need to teach them the family values of love and acceptance, even for those with whom they disagree. And when children act hatefully, punish them, not the targets of their hatred.

Punishing gays and their children for the homophobia of others makes as much sense as punishing a robbery victim or a rape victim. Children learn hatred from their parents, and many of those children grow up to commit discrimination and hate crimes.

By repeating misinformation about gays and by spitefully using words like "faggot," you encourage your children to taunt or assault the targets of your bigotry. If your children happen to be gay, your actions can cause them to hate themselves and any reflections of themselves in others; thus, you might encourage them to commit violence against themselves or other gays. Stop the cycle of hatred and violence, instead of contributing to it. I think responsible parents who happen to disapprove of homosexuals should qualify that disapproval in terms that also show their disapproval of violence, harassment, and suicide; otherwise, they might have blood on their hands.

Of course children will get teased. Children get teased. But the children of gays are tougher than you might think. They've formed various support networks, especially through the internet. Groups like Colage (Children of Lesbians and Gays Everywhere) and Family Pride offer shared resources and experience for gays and their children, including the grown children of gays. So do publications like *Alternative Family Magazine*.

Instead of making broad generalizations from a few isolated cases, and instead of simply repeating made-up statistics, many researchers have looked at actual children of various gay couples, and found that they tend to be no more or less mentally balanced than other children. You can find some of the research in books like the following: *Reinventing The Family: The Emerging Story Of Lesbian And Gay Parents* (by Laura Benkov), *The Lesbian Parenting Book: A Guide to Creating Families and Raising Children* (by D. Merilee Clunis and G. Dorsey Green),

*Families of Value: Gay and Lesbian Parents and Their Children Speak Out* (by Jane Drucker), *Zack's Story: Growing Up With Same-Sex Parents* (by Keith Elliot Greenberg and photographer Carol Halebian), *The Lesbian and Gay Parenting Handbook: Creating and Raising Our Families* (by April Martin), *Out of the Ordinary: Essays on Growing Up With Gay, Lesbian, and Transgender Parents* (edited by Noelle Howey and Ellen Samuels), *Families Like Mine: Children of Gay Parents Tell It Like It Is* (by Abigail Garner), and *Growing Up in a Lesbian Family: Effects on Child Development* (Fiona L. Tasker and Susan Golombok).

As if we didn't experience enough special discrimination against gays, some politicians keep trying to pass laws that single out gays as unfit for adoption. The politicians who win money and votes by promoting those laws and playing on people's fears will never mention that the laws (1) use up millions of taxpayer dollars that would otherwise have gone to investigating child abuse, (2) sometimes involve witch hunts of current foster parents, (3) sometimes over-ride a deceased person's will, (4) take children from their homes, and (5) strand children in orphanages. Those politicians also fail to mention that gay foster parents have a strong tendency to adopt someone that no one else wanted, such as babies born with drug addiction or HIV, and (let's face the racism here) African American babies.

The sponsoring politicians care more about looking heroic than admitting to those terrible by-products of anti-gay adoption laws. Apparently, they just want money, votes, and a pat on the back from powerful anti-gay lobbyists.

# "GOD SENT AIDS TO THE HOMOSEXUALS BECAUSE HE LOVES HIS CHILDREN AND WANTS TO TURN THEM BACK TO HIM."

Do you love your children? If so, would you give them AIDS as a way of turning them back to you? Out of love, would you kill them for disobeying you? No? Then what makes you think that your power to love, forgive, and accept your children is stronger than God's? If they came down with a disease, and you could save them with a transfusion of your blood, I doubt you would say, "I won't save your life unless you agree to obey all my rules from now on."

The "curse on gays" reasoning makes God look awfully clumsy. After all, He keeps giving AIDS to unborn children, to hospital patients, and to the faithful wives of unfaithful men. He also gives it to heterosexual women much more than to lesbians. You would think someone as powerful and resourceful as God could create a better queer-seeking missile. God also must hate teens, elderly people, and people of color, because He gives HIV to more minorities (especially blacks) than whites, as well as to an ever-increasing number of teens and the elderly. If AIDS is a curse from God, does God like lesbians more than heterosexual women or whites more than blacks, Asians, and Hispanics? Of course, I don't really believe God hates people or "gives" people AIDS, but I wanted to show the flaw in that thinking.

Instead of seeing HIV as God's punishment on gays, we need to look at the failure of gays and nongays alike to fully address this health-care crisis. Should we think of it as godly to let people die alone, to disown your children when they need you most, to suppress information that could protect the general public, to delight in the death of others as a supposed validation of your theological stance, or to give children the false and dangerous impression that AIDS can't reach heterosexuals? Of course, just as heterosexuals need to quit blaming HIV completely on gays or attributing it to God's will, we can't give heterosexuals all the blame either. Much of the failure to address AIDS comes from certain gay men; their recklessness not only tarnishes the gay community but also robs society in general of far too many talented men.

Thoughtlessness often leads to AIDS. That thoughtlessness might come from the gay teenager who spends his money on crystal meth but never bothers with condoms, or from the heterosexual legislator who couldn't care less how many people die when he passes that law banning condom discussion or needle exchanges. After all, the boy gets his kicks not only from sex but also from crystal and other mind-altering drugs that make him even more sexually reckless. After all, the legislator gets re-elected for his supposed protecting of the family; never mind that he fails to protect the many families losing people to AIDS. We also see thoughtlessness from certain governments, who allow HIV-tainted blood to continue circulating in hospitals, or who keep banning, twisting, or suppressing HIV education.

But remember that those are people spreading AIDS and people refusing to address the spread of AIDS. Don't blame God. If God killed all the people who label each other sinners, Earth would run out of people immediately.

# "GOD DIDN'T CREATE ADAM AND STEVE."

If we take Genesis literally, as a statement of proper sexual behavior, it endorses incest. After all, whom could Cain and Abel marry but their sisters, and whom could Adam and Eve's grandchildren marry but each other? If Adam and Eve were the only two people God created, how did Cain manage to find a wife when he went into exile? Why was God worried about other people not recognizing Cain as the son of Adam and Eve, if Adam and Eve were the only parents and their children were the only other people? Who else was on Earth to not recognize him? Who made all those other people? Considering the extraordinary circumference of Earth, God must have made a lot of other people, if Cain just happened to bump into some of them. Maybe some of the other people God created were gay. While many people of faith can offer reasonable answers to those questions, most such answers show a more complex mentality and interpretation than making vapid comments like "God didn't create Adam and Steve." Why not use that same intelligent reasoning when dealing with gay issues?

As I illustrate with "If: A Satire" (later in this book), a literal reading of Genesis also fails to account for disabilities, the different races, and many other human variances, so why use it against gays? Which color were Adam and Eve? Many white people will assume Adam and Eve were white, just as many whites become uneasy (and some even become violent) if a black actor plays Jesus. If we see Adam, Eve, and Jesus as white, does that make it unnatural to be a person of color? Keep in mind that racists use parts of Genesis to promote their bigotry agenda, particularly the odd little story where Noah curses his son for accidentally seeing him drunk and naked. Not surprisingly, racist groups and even sexist groups tend to overlap with the groups who consider themselves brilliant and original when they make the tired "Adam and Steve" comment.

I think Genesis just establishes that God sees both men and women as His children, His creation. He loves all human beings: Hispanic, Native American, gay, deaf, left-handed, diabetic, fat, skinny, whatever. By referring separately to men and women, the Genesis accounts cover all human beings—not just white male heterosexual Republican fundamentalist Christians with no disabilities. We could read Genesis as meaning we should all live as Adam and Eve clones, but I think it simply means that we should see all people as God's children. If God created all people, then God created Adam and Steve, and anyone who says "God didn't create Adam and Steve" is saying that God didn't create all people. Peter J. Gomes, preacher to Harvard University, makes many important clarifications about the Bible's words and misuses in his thoughtful study *The Good Book*; one of those clarifications is that the Bible's omission of gays from the creation accounts hardly means the same as condemning gays.

We could also take the Adam and Eve story as saying that humans only exist to reproduce, but that wouldn't explain why Jesus and Paul both said that not everyone should marry (Matthew 19:12; I Corinthians 7:1–8), or why God sent Eve mostly for something either gender can provide: companionship (Genesis 2:18). It certainly fails to tackle Jesus' condoning discussion of the three types of eunuchs, including those born unable to reproduce (also in Matthew 19:12), or the fact that the Bible refers to many of its heroes as eunuchs. If God sees it as evil for any human being not to reproduce, what makes the Bible show Jesus, Paul, and eunuchs in such a favorable light? If you see Jesus as our ultimate role model and reproduction as our most divine purpose, why didn't Jesus get married and have children, and why did He encourage others to avoid marriage and reproduction? His message focused not on making as many people as possible but on helping and loving the people we encounter, a point that many of His followers tend to ignore.

# "THE BIBLE SAYS IT'S WRONG."

If we want to take some Leviticus verses literally and out of context, what about the ones saying not to eat fruit from a young tree (19:23), read horoscopes (19:26), get a haircut (19:27), get a beard trim (19:27), get a tattoo (19:28), eat shellfish (11:9–12), eat meat with fat or blood (3:17), touch a menstruating woman or anything she touches (15:19–33), crossbreed cattle (19:19), plant two different kinds of seed in the same field (19:19), wear clothing of mixed fabric (19:19), eat pork (11:7–8), touch pigskin (11:8), or have sex with a woman "having her sickness" (20:18)? What about some verses outside Leviticus, like the ones saying not to use profanity (Colossians 3:8), act out of anger (Psalms 37:8), get drunk (Pr. 20:1), pray aloud in public (Matthew 6:1–8), swear (Matthew 5:34), call someone worthless or a fool (Matthew 5:22), charge interest to poor people (Ex. 22:25), judge people (Matthew 7:1–5), or hate people (I John 4:20)? Should we follow the verse saying that no one should make a newlywed man work or serve his country for the first year of his marriage (Deuteronomy 24:5)?

Should women see their menstruation cycles as "sin" (Leviticus 15:19–33)? Should women see it as sinful to bear a male child, and even more sinful to bear a female child (Leviticus 12:1–8)? Should women follow the New Testament passages where Paul says they must always remain "silent" and "under obedience" while at church (I Corinthians 14:34), that they can't put braids in their hair or certain jewels around their neck (I Timothy 2:9), that they must pray with their heads covered (I Corinthians 11:5), that they are inferiors who caused the fall of humanity (I Timothy 2:13–14), that they can only redeem themselves by bearing children (I Timothy 2:15), and that they cannot teach or "usurp authority over the man" (I Timothy 2:12)? Should we follow Exodus 21:7 in its guidance on how a daughter should act when her parents sell her into slavery?

What about the verses that require churches to pay taxes (Romans 14:6–7; Matthew 22:21; Luke 20:25)? Should we also follow the biblical tradition of promoting slavery (Leviticus 25:44–46; Ephesians 6:5), or the one of keeping the disabled from our places of worship (Leviticus 21:18–23)? Should we bring back the death penalty for people who work on the Sabbath (Exodus 35:2), people who use God's name in vain (Leviticus 24:16), anyone who commits adultery (Leviticus 20:10), a woman who loses her virginity before marriage (Deuteronomy 22:13–21), a son who acts stubbornly or rebelliously (Deuteronomy 21:18–21), and "everyone who curses his father or his mother" (Leviticus 20:9)?

Too many people scream Bible verses that condemn others, but find ways to disregard verses that condemn themselves. The famous list of hell-bound sinners in Romans 1 covers every person ever born (anyone who ever lies, gossips, acts out of anger, holds a grudge, starts arguments, etc.), but the idea of certain actions causing damnation conflicts with John 3:16–17. In context, Paul used the list to show that no one should judge, because we all face condemnation by someone's standards (Romans 2:1). If gays will burn in Hell for violating the list, won't everyone else? Also keep in mind Paul's admission (I Corinthians 7:6, 7:25, etc.) that parts of the letters we now read only came from his opinion; of course, Paul didn't realize that the letters he wrote to disciples and churches would find their way into the Bible. Another of Paul's lists appears in I Corinthians 6:10, in which he said anyone who gets drunk, has premarital sex, cheats others, or envies others will go to Hell, but most people use ellipses in place of those references, so they can safely and self-righteously quote the same passage's references to gay sex.

In fact, the Bible only mentions man/man sex three-twelve times (depending on the particular translation we choose and how we choose to interpret the individual passages) and woman/woman sex one time, while condemning idolatrous man/woman sex around 360 times. How odd that so many readers can overlook something constant in favor of something that occurs only a few times! Biblical condemnations of self-righteousness, divorce, gossip, and drunkenness each separately surpass the condemnations of gay sex in their frequency, yet most people still overlook those many in favor of the few that seem to refer to gay sex.

Some will point out that Leviticus deems male/male sex "an abomination," but it says the same about eating pigs, oysters, clams, shrimp, rabbits, and many other creatures in Leviticus 20:25, a passage where the author clearly shows that he only uses "abomination" to mean "unclean" or "vulgar" by Hebrew holiness code standards—i.e., not kosher. I've yet to meet anyone who even tries to follow the entire Hebrew holiness code, so why elevate two verses from it? Keep in mind also that Proverbs 6:16–19 lists several of what Solomon calls "abominations" to God, including three "abominations" that many televangelists and politicians practice constantly: arrogance, deceit, and divisiveness. Solomon, in his wisdom, left same-gender sex out of his "abominations" list. Furthermore, the Bible says that anyone who claims to follow the law but breaks any one part of it is breaking all of it (James 2:10), so a man who lives by the law but eats pork is also guilty of lying with a man as with a woman; the Bible offers only guilt for people who live by the law instead of living by grace.

Though surrounded by the openly bisexual Roman culture, Christ never mentioned same-gender relations; instead, He taught people about love and acceptance, even going out of His way to meet the rejected half-breeds of Samaria. Yes, He mentioned heterosexual relationships, but He never condemned gay ones.

Some people say that His condemnation of adultery automatically included homosexuality, but the Bible offers no support for that definition of adultery; according to scripture, adultery meant having sex with someone other than one's first sex partner (Genesis 2:24; Matthew 5:32, 19:9; Mark 10:11–12).

His only possible reaction to homosexuality occurred when He healed the "pais" of a centurion (Matthew 8:5–13). Though the King James Bible renders it "servant," the word "pais" might also have carried gay connotations at that time—a connotation strengthened both by the prevalence of open bisexuality in ancient Roman culture and by the obvious love between this particular centurion and servant. Christ reacted to the centurion's love by healing the servant. Notice, however, that Christ made no judgment of this relationship. Daniel A. Helminiak, a Roman Catholic priest, examines various studies of that passage, and of all the supposedly anti-gay passages, in his book *What the Bible Really Says About Homosexuality*. I recommend that book for further study.

Of course, many people will go beyond specific passages and use the Bible to make a blanket statement about homosexuality as "an immoral lifestyle." Using that tendency to take scriptures out of context and impose them on others, consider how Jesus said that anyone who marries a divorced person commits adultery (Matthew 5:32, 19:9; Mark 10:11–12). Therefore, by those standards, a divorced person in a second marriage lives an immoral lifestyle, and anyone who supports that marriage supports sin. With that in mind, it seems hypocritical that many divorced and remarried people will claim gays pose a threat to family values, religious values, and the institution of marriage.

We could even accuse people who support football teams or sell pork of promoting an immoral lifestyle (Leviticus 11:7–8). We could even say female Sunday school teachers live an immoral lifestyle (I Corinthians 14:34–35).

We could also say churchgoers promote an immoral lifestyle by filling up restaurants, donut shops, and grocery stores on Sundays, forcing employees to violate the Sabbath. Many people who work on Sundays consider themselves Christians, though your way of thinking suggests that they live an immoral lifestyle. Actually, the Bible places the Sabbath on Friday night and Saturday morning, but most fundamentalists overlook that faltering from the letter, as well as the fact that Jesus and his disciples violated the Sabbath.

Besides prayerfully and closely reading the Bible all the way through several times, I have found a great deal of help in understanding its applications to gays, thanks to books like *Things They Never Told You In Sunday School: A Primer For The Christian Homosexual* (by David Day), *The New Testament and Homosexuality* (by Robin Scroggs), and many of the other resources I mention in "Reactions to Homophobia." Those works helped me form some of the following observations about Christianity, specifically the idea of Biblical literalism.

Jesus criticized the Pharisees for their attempts at wearing the best clothing, particularly during worship services (Matthew 23:5; Mark 12:38–39). As His "lilies of the field" allegory shows, Christ preferred simple, perfunctory clothing that reflected only the practical concern of covering oneself (Matthew 6:28–34). Yet, countless churches today follow an unwritten code that everyone must wear their so-called "Sunday best," turning the church aisle into a fashion runway. Even on the hottest days, men in such churches will wear three-piece suits, while the women overdress in uncomfortable-looking fashions. So much for the humility and pragmatism that Jesus taught.

Back to more relevant matters, Jesus and His disciples promoted racial harmony and interaction, welcoming Greeks and people of interracial heritage to break bread with them. Yet, many white congregations still prefer whites only in their buildings, while using out-of-context Bible verses to condemn interracial dating and interracial marriage. Some churches still use the Bible to show blacks as inferior or cursed.

I even heard the word "nigger" casually used during church or Sunday school in my original home state of Louisiana; as you can guess, the racial slurs really started flying after those churchgoers left holy ground. I've also heard racism and racial slurs from churchgoers in my temporary home state Tennessee and my permanent home state Texas, but not with the same fanatical frequency as in Louisiana, and not while inside the church building.

Whenever I see it, I attribute religion-based homophobia and religion-based racism to bigotry, not to God. At this point, let me clarify that I am attacking bigotry, not God or Christianity. Further, I am not calling homosexuality a sin, but showing the problem with using out-of-context verses as a way to label gays as sinful and thus somehow deserving of discrimination, violence, etc. With that said, I want to further expose the idolatrous worship of tradition.

We see that worship when many Christians become riled over newer Bible translations using gender-neutral language in place of male-specific language, even though the translators will say the gender-neutral language more closely follows the actual texts. Tradition replaced the Bible's original phrasing, so tradition-worshippers will claim sacrilege when someone brings back the original phrasing. In that case and in the Sodom and Gomorrah passage I'll soon discuss, tradition actually outweighs scripture for many Christians.

Good or bad, tradition affects our thinking, including our theology. Christians need to quit confusing Christian tradition with the Bible and the Bible with

God. By definition of monotheistic religion (worship of only one God), Christians should not worship tradition, the Bible, or anything else but God. Reconciling Trinitarian doctrine with monotheism (i.e., explaining how Father, Son, and Holy Ghost form the one and only God) poses enough problems without us seeing the Bible as also a part of God. Many people speak of God and the Bible as if they were equal, and hold their Bibles as if they were touching the hand of God. When we stop confusing tradition and the Bible with God, we can begin a deeper examination of what the Bible really says.

That examination also requires going beyond what certain, selected verses literally say. Reading the Bible literally requires disregarding scientific and historic evidence. For example, we would need to see the Earth as created in seven literal days (and not the Bible's later concept of equating God's days with a thousand of ours), see the Earth as only 6000–35,000 years old, and see all types of life-form evolution as nonexistent.

The Sermon on the Mount also presents too many problems for Christian fundamentalists. I challenge anyone to read Matthew chapters 5–8 aloud, stopping after each verse to ask "Do I even try to literally follow that?" I'm not saying that you try and fail; I'm saying that you probably don't even try to follow many of those verses. Jesus later claimed that we should rid ourselves of our hands, feet, and eyes if they might cause us to sin (Matthew 18:8–9). Since most Christian fundamentalists somehow manage to keep their hands, feet, and eyes, we can assume either that they never face temptation, or that they fail to take that passage literally. The second assumption seems more plausible.

Jesus even pulled His followers away from literalism by constantly speaking in parables. Should we read the parables literally? Read literally or figuratively, I think all the teachings of Jesus come down to five points: (1) laws can save no one, (2) love matters more than all the other laws, (3) acts of compassion impress God more than religious displays, (4) we cannot truly love God unless we also love all human beings, (5) those who believe in and accept Jesus Christ as their Savior shall receive salvation. Those five points emphasize Christianity as a life of love, peace, volunteerism, and hope, while many Christians downplay those concepts in favor of reducing the Bible into a tool for judging and controlling others.

If you're a Christian, I challenge you to allow for metaphor, balance, opinion, and context when reading the Bible. We should acknowledge the difficulty of translating from one language to another, especially when the translators tried to precisely translate a book written in four ancient languages over a period of hundreds or even thousands of years. In many cases, the translators could not find more than one use of a particular archaic word. Still, they supposedly translated that word accurately. Many people who have read the Bible in its ancient languages will admit that all the translations contain errors, so why should we assume that the parts about gay sex were translated correctly?

Reading your holy book requires not always reading it literally, but always reading it with the idea that one must continue learning and seeking in order to continue one's constant journey toward a deeper understanding of spiritual matters. You extinguish the discovery process when you claim that you already fully understand every aspect of a book and that no misreading or textual friction could possibly exist.

Challenges to total literalism often invoke a recital of platitudes, instead of an examination of the verses I just mentioned. Platitudes get us nowhere, and they certainly can't help the many people who become the targets of the many fanatical fundamentalists who commit, encourage, or ignore hate crimes. At some point, we need to start questioning fundamentalist rigidity in favor of compassion and free thought. When people reject, mistreat, assault, or murder each other for not fitting into some rigid theological view, we have reached that point.

# "THE BIBLE SAYS GOD DESTROYED SODOM AND GOMORRAH BECAUSE OF GAYS."

The very term "Sodomy" comes from that deliberate misreading of scripture, one that apparently evolved long after the writing of Genesis. Ezekiel 16:49 clearly refers to the sin of Sodom as hoarding wealth but failing to help the needy; Jesus always identified the sin of Sodom as failing to welcome strangers. Therefore, the term "Sodomy" should refer to rudeness, callousness, and greed, including that of many televangelists and politicians.

Some Bible scholars see the Bible's use of words that appear to refer to homosexuality as actually a reference to male temple prostitution, an aspect of fertility rituals and Baal worship; male prostitution hardly covers or condemns all gays, just as the Bible's references to female prostitution hardly condemn all heterosexuals. In fact, many Christians believe that all the Bible's supposed condemnations of homosexuality actually appear in contexts that involve prostitution or humiliation. People in biblical times lacked a concept of sexual orientation, and we are only beginning to understand the complexities of what makes someone gay, bi, or heterosexual.

It takes a great deal of prejudice for anyone to see "prostitution" and "homosexual" as synonyms. Since the Bible actually never clarifies what "Sodomite" means, translators simply make their judgments and add their footnotes according to their biases. As proof of the word's vagueness, the translation of "Sodomite" varies wildly between all the different Bible versions. Reaching even more desperately for condemnations of gays, some people will even find biblical references to "wickedness" in ancient cities and claim "wickedness" meant homosexuality; we could just as easily claim "wickedness" meant over-eating (a taboo in Hebrew culture).

Consider Genesis chapters 14–19: how can we look at the Sodomites as bad and Lot as good? Some might argue that Lot's sins happened after God decided to destroy the two cities, so those didn't affect his "good man" status, but the supposed gay rape story also didn't happen until after God's decision. And just what were Lot's sins? Lot got drunk two nights in a row, impregnating one of his daughters each of those two nights. Of course, that happened after he offered those daughters to strangers for rape.

Yes, Genesis says that some people wanted to "know" the angels, and "know" might have meant they wanted to commit rape. But why confuse same-gender rape with consenting gay sex, or with a committed gay relationship? Would we also confuse heterosexual rape with consenting heterosexual intercourse or relationships?

In his insightful book *Openly Gay Openly Christian*, Rev. Samuel Kader examines the original wording of that passage to prove that "know" probably didn't mean "rape" or "have sex with," that the people who wanted to "know" the angels probably weren't all men, and that those people probably hadn't seen the visitors or realized that they were male. Kader sees no trace of homosexuality in that passage or similar passages about destroyed cities. Because of certain footnotes that mention gays, he also states the obvious but overlooked point that Bible readers should not see footnotes in a Bible translation as an actual part of the Bible. Daniel A. Helminiak, in his book *What the Bible Really Says About Homosexuality*, argues that the passage does indeed refer to rape, but that it still does not mean God destroyed the cities for homosexuality.

Was every citizen of both cities a gay man? If so, who propagated, and why would Lot bother to invite gay men to rape his virgin daughters? If not, why didn't God spare the cities, or at least let the heterosexuals escape? God said He would spare the city for ten righteous people (Genesis 18:32); if righteous meant "not gay," surely any city has at least ten heterosexuals. Should we really believe that Lot was the only heterosexual out of all those people?

Assuming the children were born gay contradicts the notion of saying gays choose to be gay. Otherwise, how could we look at the children as gay, and why would God not spare them? What made God kill all those children? Some claim the nongays died for failing to condemn the gays, but how could a newborn child condemn anyone? I know that diseases, accidents, and natural disasters are neither good nor evil in their violence, but how could a good and loving God purposefully kill a baby? One more question…if we see Lot as the only good person, why let his wife and daughters leave with him? The Bible never refers to them as good; in fact, it shows all three of them as disobedient to God.

Maybe the author of Genesis mistakenly saw the destruction of Sodom and Gomorrah as God's wrath, but it really only represented some natural disaster that the author could not understand, such as an asteroid or tornado. We make the same mistake when we refer to natural disasters as "God's will" or "an act of God," instead of trying to reduce human losses from those disasters. We can't prevent natural disasters (not yet, anyway), but architects, city planners, educators, and others can prevent many of the human losses, instead of resigning themselves to passivity and saying that "God decided it was time for those people to go." In the same manner, the Bible's writers tended to view all events as God's will, rather than blaming nature or humanity.

Still, even if we accept it as historically accurate and read it completely literally, the Bible never says God destroyed any cities because of gays. Never. Not because of gays only. Not because of gays and other reasons. Simply not because of gays.

The Sodomy hoax reveals how churches, like the Pharisees, often take creative license with scripture in order to create more sins and feel more holy. It turns into the worship of tradition, an idolatry I mentioned before. We can find other examples of that worship. The Bible shows dancing as serving important religious and social functions, but many churches and some religious colleges forbid dancing. Contrary to what countless Protestant churches tell us, the Bible condemns getting drunk but condones moderate drinking.

Aside from Pentecostals, Assemblies of God, and certain non-denominational churches, most churches actually consider it heresy to speak in tongues, though the Bible encourages speaking in tongues; Paul even said "forbid not to speak with tongues" (I Corinthians 14:39). If Paul only referred to people in that time, could his same-gender passages have only referred to people in that time?

The Bible refers to adultery as having sex with a married person or even a divorced person, but many churches let adultery exclude divorced people and include all gay sex. Some churches even grant themselves the option to pretend a particular marriage never even happened, simply by declaring the marriage "annulled."

People who take such liberties with the Bible certainly have no business using its verses literally and out of context against gays. But when they do, they could at least avoid using made-up, passed-down claims like "The Bible says God destroyed Sodom and Gomorrah because of gays."

# "I LOVE THE SINNER, HATE THE SIN."

Prove it. Listen to gay issues from a gay perspective; speak out against hate crimes; invite gay friends to the movies or a restaurant; sincerely say "I love you" to a gay friend. Avoid turning red and screaming the same few Bible verses at gays, because a lot of us know how the textual and historical contexts change their meanings. A lot of us also read the verses that apply to the people who use the Bible against gays.

For example, if the Bible endorses homophobia, then please explain why St. John made so many statements like the following: "There is no fear in love; but perfect love casteth out fear: because fear hath torment. He that feareth is not made perfect in love" (I John 4:18). St. John's thinking, like that of Christ, runs counter to the fear and hatred promoted by homophobic and/or racist groups. However, such groups usually obfuscate that fear and hatred with patriotic and religious rhetoric, or phrases like "I love the sinner, hate the sin."

What kind of doublespeak allows you to love gays and to avoid their company? People who love each other want to spend time together; that includes fundamentalists who supposedly love their gay children. You might say that God wants Christians to avoid so-called "bad people," but Jesus and His disciples made a point of eating and drinking with people they saw as immoral. And please explain this mythical separation of sin from sinner, personality from person, life from lifestyle, hatred from hated, homosexuality from homosexual.

Please explain why so many people call gays "sinners" but overlook other so-called "sins." Please explain why those people focus on gays so much more than on any other group the Bible might seem to condemn. Why not make videos like *The Divorced People's Agenda*, *The Judgmental People's Agenda*, etc.? Why not stage demonstrations and boycotts that target lying, hate crimes, corporate downsizing, sweatshops, or domestic violence? Why do you keep condemning us when you refuse to condemn hate crimes? Saying "I don't condone violence" when we put someone on the spot isn't the same as speaking out against violence. The KKK and other white supremacist groups also claim that they "don't condone violence," so how seriously should we take that feeble denunciation?

How can anyone compare supposed loved ones to kleptomaniacs, alcoholics, murderers, child molesters, and Satan? How can anyone refer to supposed loved ones as "darkness, sick, twisted, perverts, demons, devil-possessed, freaks, trash, filth, blights, degenerates, monsters, lifestyle, deathstyle, issue, anti-family, hell-spawns, threats, predators, animals, fruitcakes, a curse, a disease, the world," etc.?

It would sound more loving if everyone referred to us as their brothers, sisters, and children; it would also reflect reality.

If you come down with an illness, we can blame it on your so-called "lifestyle choice," call you horrible names, deny you your civil rights, refuse to let your spouse visit you in the hospital, tell you that you'll burn in Hell, and remind you that we love the sinner, hate the sin. When you die, we'll lie to everyone about what killed you, we'll refuse to include the cause of death in your obituary, we'll refuse to let your spouse or friends come to the funeral, we'll make sure your spouse receives none of your property or benefits, we'll try to take anything your spouse co-owned with you, and we might even try to take your spouse's belongings. Hopefully, we wouldn't actually treat you that way, but many nongays treat us that way while shouting scripture at us, and it looks nothing like love.

Fortunately, many people of faith show love and acceptance of gays, and see nothing wrong with homosexuality, as I show in the next section of this essay. Those people exist across many belief systems, all over Earth.

However, many other people of faith fall into a third category that gays and nongays alike often fail to acknowledge. Those particular religious persons happen to see homosexuality as a sin but still feel and live a calling to treat gays with dignity, respect, and…yes…love. I can agree to disagree with those people, enjoying their friendship and benefiting from their support. We learn from each other and help each other, instead of pretending to know everything or not need each other.

I disagree with everyone about certain issues, just as everyone disagrees with everyone else about certain issues. But let's take the focus off the hatred.

Sincerely show love, and more people will listen to you. They might not agree, but at least they'll listen. That's all you can ask, and all I ask.

# "ANYONE WHO CONDONES HOMOSEXUALITY CAN'T BE RELIGIOUS OR MORAL."

Not having your morals isn't the same as not having any morals. Do you agree, as the Bible says in Leviticus 11:7–8, that it's an abomination to eat pork? Many people do. If you don't agree, how can you claim to have any morals? If that question makes no sense, please quit using the same logic for your homophobic remarks.

Many people consider it a sin to drink alcohol in any quantity, date or marry outside one's race or religion, work during the Sabbath, get a divorce, marry a divorced person, read a horoscope, or allow a woman to hold any sort of leadership position within a church. The Bible can back all those beliefs if, like you, we learn to magnify certain out-of-context verses. By your logic, disagreeing with any of those beliefs means that you lack morals and cannot judge right from wrong.

Morality and spirituality can exist with or without each other. Many atheists have strong moral codes, while many people of faith commit unspeakable crimes. The inverse is also true. If religion blocks immorality, what makes terrorists and other individuals commit violence in the name of religion, and how can you explain the thievery, oppression, child molestation, and other problems sometimes perpetrated by certain people who hold religious office? You might claim that being moral requires believing in a literal interpretation (i.e., your literal interpretation) of both the Old and New Testament. Yet, many people of faiths other than Christianity are highly moral, just as many of them are highly immoral. Even St. Paul, who often seemed obsessed with purity issues, made clear distinctions between morality and spirituality, appearance and sincerity, works and faith.

Many people's religious and/or philosophical convictions cause them to see it as immoral to eat animals. Some cultures consider it immoral for a woman to reveal her face in public; some other cultures see nothing immoral about a woman revealing her breasts at a beach; and still other cultures see nothing immoral about any public nudity. Everyone seems immoral or amoral by someone's standards, but I've never met anyone who doesn't live by some moral code. I certainly wouldn't agree with all the moral codes in the world, and I certainly wouldn't say that nothing is wrong or evil. Still, I can have morals without embracing all of your stances on right and wrong.

Those who use certain scriptural passages literally and out of context to condemn gays cannot honestly represent the views of all people of faith. In fact, religions disagree with each other over a number of moral issues, and a great deal of moral disagreement occurs within each religion, each denomination, each place of worship, etc.

The first Metropolitan Community Church (MCC) congregation started in California from the need for a gay-friendly church. Today, the churches in that denomination represent the diversity so often rejected by others, joining people of different races, sexual orientations, religious backgrounds, etc. As MCC explains in its brochures and Web pages, the Bible contains some loving, same-gender relationships (Jonathan and David, Naomi and Ruth, etc.) that surpassed the love those people held for any member of the opposite gender. The Bible never refers to these people having gay sex, but many heterosexuals now use the words of Ruth to Naomi (Ruth 1:16–17) as wedding vows, which seems to suggest Ruth married Naomi. Also, David and Jonathan sounded like more than friends at times, such as when David said, "I am distressed for thee, my brother Jonathan: very pleasant hast thou been unto me: thy love to me was wonderful, passing the love of women" (II Samuel 1:26). Also see Daniel 1:9; I Samuel 18:1–5, 20:41; and II Samuel 20:3–4.

The United Churches of Christ and the Society of Friends (Quakers) also welcome LGBTs without clarification. Though national Episcopalian leadership still splits on the issue, the individual congregations in that faith often see gay as simply the way God made certain people. At the time I was finishing this essay, the national Methodist and Presbyterian leaderships both remained divided over gay issues, though many Methodist and Presbyterian churches now see homosexuality as a non-issue.

Composed of gays and their supporters, gay-friendly movements within many Christian denominations now work at a national or even international level to bring change. These groups hope not to cure LGBTs or conditionally tolerate them ("Love the sinner, hate the sin") but to welcome them into the church. A small sampling follows: Reconciling Congregations Program (Methodists), Reconciled in Christ Program (Lutheran), More Light Churches Network (Presbyterian), Open and Affirming Program (United Churches Of Christ), Dignity (Catholics), Affirmation (Mormons), Welcoming & Affirming Baptists, and Honesty (Southern Baptists).

Epitomizing hypocrisy, the Mormon church initially took a gay-friendly stance amid rumors of homosexuality within its early leadership, but that same church became anti-gay when it found gay baiting would help its image and acceptance among those Christian denominations that think of Mormons as "nonChristians" or as a cult. In other words, they tried to make friends with the big kids by finding a common enemy, by picking on some other rejected kid. Apparently, becoming a self-titled "real Christian" requires exclusivity, loathing, divisiveness, finger pointing, victimizing, gossip, deception, fear, and a denial of the past. How sad that so-called "real" Christianity fails to reflect the teachings of Christ. Of course, Mormon churches refused to ordain black priests until the 1970s, so I suppose they wanted to channel that bigotry somewhere else.

The Unitarian Universalist Church openly supports gays. As noted gay journalist Michelangelo Signorile has reported in *The Advocate*, gay Muslims can face torture or even execution in many places, but they organize and find information through various Web sites, such as the one created by the gay Muslim group Al-Fatiha (http://www.al-fatiha.org/). Buddhists remain largely split on gay issues; however, many people view Buddhism as less a religion than a philosophy, with many of its members belonging to a variety of different religions. Hinduism is largely tolerant, if not completely indifferent, over issues of sexual orientation.

Native American religions generally acknowledge gay, lesbian, or androgynous individuals as "two-spirited," blessed with both the spirit of a man and the spirit of a woman. Rather than trying to force these people into accepted gender roles, most Native Americans treated (and, where invading prejudices haven't prevailed, still treat) two-spirited people as blessings who strengthen extended families, settle conflicts within male/female relationships, offer unique perspectives, provide role models as hard workers, and often serve as spiritual leaders.

Reformed Judaism not only accepts homosexuality but also works for gay equality. Though Orthodox Judaism condemns homosexuality, many gays remain active in Orthodoxy and in trying to bring change to their faith.

Keep in mind also that scriptural interpretations and other religious views vary among gays as much as they vary among anyone else. But no one can honestly say that all religious people condemn homosexuality. Many people of faith are gay or gay-friendly, but some people try to convince everyone otherwise—that you can't be religious unless you agree with everything they say. They try to make it sound like people will go to Hell for being different from them, or even for disagreeing with them. But they aren't God, and they need reminding of that fact.

Paul said, "For whosoever shall call upon the name of the Lord shall be saved" (Romans 10:13), while Jesus said, "For God so loved the world, that he gave his only begotten Son, that whosoever believeth in him should not perish, but have everlasting life. For God sent not his Son into the world to condemn the world; but that the world through him might be saved" (John 3:16–17). Note the absence of qualifications—i.e., any heterosexuals who believe, any fundamentalists who believe, etc. Those verses and many others contradict the teachings of TV evangelists, who often make it sound like you purchase salvation by sending them money and/or earn salvation by blindly following them.

According to Christ, no one can buy, earn, or even deserve salvation; it comes from His grace. As Alexander Penman so eloquently illustrates in his ebook *Beyond Religion*, Christians who use their religious perspectives to condemn people tend to overlook God's grace in favor of their belief systems.

Will gay and gay-friendly people of faith ever change the views of people who see all their religious views as irrefutable? Unlikely, but we might convince them that those views actually call them to love the people they see as "sinners." They're entitled to their opinions, as long as they aren't hurting us.

Will we reach people who allow for interpretation or context? Possibly.

Will we reach parents who want to love their gay children but find that love at war with everything else they believe? Possibly, and we need to try, for the sake of the parents and their children.

Will we reach some of the gays who buy into the lies of homophobia? I say "yes," and they need us, so gay and gay-friendly people of faith must not remain silent.

# "WE CAN'T ALLOW GAY MARRIAGES, BECAUSE TRADITION PROTECTED HETEROSEXUAL MARRIAGE AND REPRODUCTION FOR THOUSANDS OF YEARS."

Protected them from what? Gays getting married won't affect whether heterosexuals continue to marry and reproduce. Heterosexual marriage and reproduction still happen in Iceland, Sweden, Denmark, Norway, Hungary, the Netherlands, and all the other places that give gays in long-term domestic partnerships virtually the same rights as they give married heterosexual couples. They still happened in all the ancient cultures that condoned homosexual relationships. We'll wait and see if gay marriages cause Canadian heterosexuals to suddenly stop marrying or reproducing; I really doubt that will happen.

Back here in America, countless heterosexuals divorce over minutia and reproduce outside marriage. Of course, some people will attempt to blame gays for those facts. Aren't scapegoats convenient?

Also, that "tradition" argument begs the question of whether we should bring back slavery or go back to forbidding interracial marriage; both practices received protection from tradition and even the Bible. Without marriage, gay couples can't receive the equal rights of insurance benefits, joint income tax returns, inheritance, hospital visitation, and a thousand other rights that married heterosexuals often take for granted.

Some people claim that, if we let two men or two women marry, then we must let a man marry a barnyard animal or a piece of furniture. Barnyard animals...and even the most fashionable couches...can't fill out paperwork, swear oaths, pay taxes, or assume legal responsibilities, so that rules them out. We are talking about two consenting, adult, human beings here. Please stop belittling and dehumanizing gay couples with these outrageous scenarios.

Though many gays will passionately disagree with me on this point, I wouldn't care if we called it something other than marriage, as long as we received the same rights as nongays. It won't hurt your marriage in any way. How can someone else's marriage possibly cause yours to fail? I can't imagine someone saying, "Honey, Bill just married Bob, so we have to get a divorce." Marriage doesn't need protecting. It needs nurturing, but not protecting; nurturing your marriage is your responsibility, not mine. I'm not responsible for the success or failure of your marriage, and I refuse to serve as your scapegoat if your marriage falters.

You might even like to say that "gays are a threat to the fabric of society." However, you reserve such elegant and ominous phrases for special occasions, such as when you fear losing a ludicrous argument, or when someone exposes your slanted statistics. The term "society" refers to people living among and depending upon each other. Though you might not realize it, many of the people you live among and depend upon are queer, queer, queer! That song on the radio, that movie you love, that car you drive, that painting in your dining room, those clothes you wear—all of those might be due in part or in full to the contributions of homosexuals. And the male organists in countless churches…I'm here to tell you, from experience, that some of them frequent gay bars on Saturday night, and that the people who couldn't figure out their orientation are in serious denial.

Unless every single person finds a desert island and moves there forever, society will continue. And guess what? Most people would refuse that desert-island approach. We need each other. Gays are a part of the fabric of society, just like you. Even violent people are a part, but even they can't destroy it. Nothing can destroy it, as long as humanity exists. Society has endured draughts, tornadoes, earthquakes, terrorism, the plague, the Crusades, polyester, and karaoke. Surely it won't collapse because you found out that Aunt Betty is a big lesbian.

Homophobia is an irrational fear or hatred of homosexuality and homosexuals. Just listen to the irrational fear in the statement that "Gays are a threat to the fabric of society." Listen to it in another stand-by: "Gays threaten the very foundation of marriage." I'm just not a big enough drama queen to believe such statements, but they get less dramatic and more personal.

For example, some people say that gay marriage and even gay relationships mock heterosexual couples. Generally, two gays become a couple because they fall in love, not because they want to mock anyone or play house. The idea of a dominating man and a submissive woman comes from a sexist society, and many couples (gay or nongay) reject such degrading notions. A gay couple might include a femme and a butch, two equally masculine people, two equally feminine people, or two people who find the whole femme/butch dichotomy limiting, insulting, and absurd.

As Una Fahy explains so well in her book *How To Make The World A Better Place For Gays And Lesbians*, it hurts gays when their nongay loved ones exclude their partners from invitations—a practice rarely used against male/female couples. Can you imagine marrying someone, but then your parents saying you can't bring your spouse to any family gathering? Can you imagine going to those gatherings alone, watching your siblings' spouses act like and feel like part of the family? Can you imagine that division of your heart, that requirement to keep your spouse away from the other people you love most? Can you imagine them treating your spouse like some monster that might emerge from the dungeon if they enter your home?

We are human, and our love is just as real as the love you hold for your spouse. That love exists in its own right and on its own terms, not as a mockery of anything. Why does it scare you so much to see a relationship that differs from yours? Even if you can't agree with letting us marry, please at least acknowledge that we can love each other, feel devoted to each other, and need to attend certain functions together as a couple.

But that's when it really scares a lot of people: when they witness us living our everyday lives, with white picket fences and the works. When they stop seeing the clown or the stereotype, we become human and harder to demonize. Why should the idea of us loving each other and wanting to commit to each other frighten anyone?

You might see gay marriage as unnatural, and it is…for heterosexuals. It's also unnatural for gays to enter into fake, heterosexual marriages; that deceit usually leads to pain for everyone involved. Why subject them to such dishonest traditions? Should we see living a lie as natural? Should we put the heterosexual spouse through such a deceitful, hollow, and cruel ordeal?

Do you get a sick feeling in your stomach when you think of gays marrying? If so, why? We all struggle with intolerance against some group, but please keep struggling with it, instead of letting it consume you. It might give you some sort of satisfaction to think that anyone who differs from you in any way is "sick" or "confused." It might even make you feel good now and then to say that you feel sorry for anyone who's different from you. But those moments of self-satisfaction won't stop hatred from eating you up inside. Hatred might seem natural, but it isn't healthy—not for you or the targets of that hatred. It might even lead you to discrimination or violence. Would you feel good about that? Of course not! Don't let hatred hurt you or others. Face it, confront it, and defeat it.

Our love poses no threat to you or your love. If two consenting adults want to commit to each other, that shouldn't scare you. And it shouldn't encourage you to set the sickening, frightening precedent of adding discrimination to the Constitution of the United States of America, a document historically used to add freedom. Equality and freedom are basic American principles, not threats to your marriage.

Please focus on more imperative issues, such as violence, health care, retirement finances, education, etc., instead of the fact that two consenting adults down the street want to get married. It's important to them, but no danger to you. The love between two men or two women poses no menace to society, or to heterosexual marriage.

# "Public schools need to quit hiring gays and quit promoting homosexuality."

I've met so many gay teachers that teaching seems like the number one gay profession—way past beauticians, antiques dealers, florists, soldiers, actors, ice skaters, dancers, and truck drivers. If someone outed all the gay teachers, and the school boards subsequently fired them (as innumerable school boards have done after individual outings), America would experience a teacher shortage like never before.

We've all had gay teachers, but few or none of them came out to us, and we were probably too naïve to realize their orientation. The ones teaching on the college level or the ones living in a select few cities might dare to come out, but even many of those people remain closeted, for job security or other reasons. And before anyone says they should just keep it to themselves, please realize that teachers, students, parents, and others will ask about their spouses or relationship status and even expect them to bring a significant other to many school-related functions. Should they lie? Also, those teachers might write about gay issues, participate in gay organizations, date someone, or live with their partner; word gets back to campus, no matter how quiet the teachers remain about their off-campus lives.

One of the most influential and inspirational teachers in your life may have been gay; how sad that you now want to take away that person's livelihood. How sad that you now want to deprive other students of the education that person gave you, the education they desperately need. What a tragic betrayal! That betrayal not only hurts the teacher but also hurts students. But the betrayal doesn't stop there; it also enters the academic regiment.

Ex-Marine Oliver Sipple serves as an example of how school boards censor history; they might allow books to mention Sipple's saving President Gerald Ford, but not that Sipple later saw his career ruined simply because people learned his sexual orientation. History textbooks remember Alan Turing's contributions: besides the fact that he greatly impacted the fields of mathematics and computer technology, his deciphering of the Enigma code helped the allies win World War II. The same books neglect to mention that his native England turned against him when the police learned his sexual orientation, or that he committed suicide after forced hormonal treatments destroyed him sexually. Famed British writer Oscar Wilde suffered a similar fate, contracting a fatal illness while serving jail time for being gay; again, most teachers and textbooks will conveniently omit those details of Wilde's life.

Teachers and textbooks will often discuss the love lives of the heterosexual historical figures they cover, but not the love lives of the gay historical figures they cover. For bisexual historical figures, only the heterosexual relationships will receive mention. For gays in a marriage of convenience (a fake and usually unconsummated marriage set up to satisfy employers, relatives, etc.), references to the hollow marriage will replace references to the person's actual love life. Even if a gay relationship lasted for decades and affected much of the historical figure's life and work, it still receives no mention.

How can we call such history accurate, when it thrives on deliberately biased omissions? Why not omit everyone's love life? Should students assume that no mention of a spouse means the person was gay?

Our educational system censors classes and textbooks, not only to keep teachers in the closet, but also to keep students from learning about gay contributions, the gays killed in the Holocaust, the executions of many gays in early America, or the acceptance of gays and transgender people among various Native American tribes. In many places, teachers who dare tell the truth about gays in history will face accusations of "promoting the homosexual lifestyle" and quickly lose their jobs.

Too many students live in fear of harassment and violence from their classmates. Much of that harassment and violence begins with someone calling a student gay, even if the particular student doesn't identify as gay or even have any homosexual desires. Gay-bashing is a problem at schools, a problem that hurts gays and nongays alike.

Teachers and administrators who want to fight the abuse might worry about facing the same "promoting the homosexual lifestyle" accusation and losing their jobs. Such measures hurt children and society, by continuing the illusion of a heterosexual world where gays should see themselves as isolated freaks that deserve to die.

Teachers who mention gay-related facts no more promote homosexuality than they promote slavery, unions, wars, zebras, rain, daffodils, Marxism, the pope, ozone depletion, or nuclear fission when they cover those topics. Giving the whole truth—the full picture—promotes nothing but truthfulness, education, informed debate, and the ability to think critically in complex situations. Giving partial truth simply amounts to lying by omission; it promotes dishonesty, ignorance, discrimination, weak debate, and an inability to cope with complex situations. We need to prepare children for the diverse world in which they will live, no matter how much that diversity frightens us. I dislike many aspects of human history, but I still need to know about those aspects. In fact, learning about something I dislike or that bothers me often benefits me even more than learning about something that I like.

Returning to teachers, though, I sometimes hear that firing teachers for being gay isn't personal, but just a way of protecting children. Supposedly, gays can serve as anything but a teacher. For familiar variations on that claim, I could cross out "teacher" to replace it with military, ministry, athletic profession, government, law enforcement field, and just about anything else. If you have nothing against us, why do you try to constrict our occupational choices? When you discriminate against us and control our lives, it shouldn't surprise you that we won't believe your "Love the sinner, hate the sin" doublespeak. When you refuse to give us the same constitutionally guaranteed rights and benefits you give others, I cannot help but see that as discrimination, and as something against us. When you try to block a qualified candidate from serving in public office only because that person happens to be gay, I can't help but think that your "anywhere but there" list won't stop with teachers.

No matter how noble your motives or how often you use the words "virtues" and "values," you can't help adult Americans by controlling how they can think, who they can love, what they can know, where they can work, what they can watch on TV, which Web sites they can visit, which books they can find in the library, which parts of history they can mention, or which jobs they can work.

Finally, I realize that teachers serve as role models, but all adults serve as role models, no matter what their occupation. Seeing gay role models might slow down the unusually high suicide rate among gay teens, something that should concern any role model. It might also discourage young people from anti-gay violence, because looking up to at least one openly gay person would cause them to see gays as human beings. However, seeing gays as human beings won't magically transform anyone into a homosexual. Nongay role models never changed the fact that I'm gay; gay role models won't turn anyone gay.

# "GAYS CAN'T JOIN FRATERNITIES AND SORORITIES, BECAUSE GREEK TRADITIONS FOLLOW THE BIBLE."

I might take that one seriously if more Greeks rejected pledges who get drunk, get tattoos, or have pre-marital sex—practices strictly condemned by the Bible. Strangely, the most homophobic, holier-than-thou remarks on college campuses often come from people who are usually too drunk to throw the first stone, including many Greeks. Also, since Greeks are so incredibly holy, why is that ads for strip joins and other adult businesses will often mention that the establishment specializes in fraternity parties? It sounds like they know their audience.

Anyone who sees gay and Greek as incompatible needs to read more history. After all, the ancient Greeks often celebrated homosexuality. Fraternities and sororities appeal to gays for obvious reasons: same-gender camaraderie, a feeling of acceptance, a sense of family, a chance to prove themselves as important contributors to society, an emphasis on community service, etc.

Countless gay Greeks remain closeted, fearful that their supposedly supportive group will suddenly reject them.

Fortunately, a group of men decided to counter the hypocrisy by starting Delta Lambda Phi, a national social fraternity for gay, bisexual, or progressive men. Some campuses also have a chapter of the lesbian sorority Lambda Delta Lambda, while other gay or gay-friendly Greek organizations continue to emerge. And, of course, many of the nongays in fraternities and sororities find homophobia offensive and unworthy of the very ideals those organizations espouse. Finally, many gays and lesbians live openly within the more long-standing Greek organizations, proving by example that being queer doesn't make someone a bad Greek...or a bad person.

# "GAYS CAN'T SERVE IN THE MILITARY, BECAUSE THAT WOULD DISRUPT EFFICIENCY."

We heard the same about women and African Americans. Different kinds of people learn to work together over time.

Keep in mind that Alexander the Great, a bisexual, conquered the known world while in his twenties, then reportedly wept for lack of more worlds to conquer. Alexander hardly sounds inefficient. He built an empire, just as other gays or bisexuals have helped create, maintain, or protect other cultures by serving in their country's military. Also consider the homosexuality within ancient Greece and its armies; surely we would not call the ancient Greek armies inefficient, especially not when our military still uses many of the warfare strategies they developed. To use a more modern example, Israel and Great Britain boast efficient armies yet openly welcome gay soldiers.

Others argue against gays in the military on the grounds of morality, but what about all the prostitutes that certain soldiers keep in business, all the illegitimate children that certain soldiers fathered in Korea and Vietnam, all the adultery scandals within the military, all the drug use or drug selling within the military, or all the women sexually harassed or assaulted by heterosexual male soldiers? Certainly, we should draw the line at rape and unwanted sexual advances, but why over something like being gay?

Still others will arrogantly assume that all gay men want all other men. Would they also assume that all heterosexual women want all men?

Some politicians falsely claim that President Bill Clinton lifted the ban on gays in the military, when he actually only codified it as "Don't ask, don't tell." The numbers of gays kicked out of the military actually increased after "Don't ask" went into effect, while the witch hunts it supposedly stopped actually continue unabated.

One manifestation of those witch-hunts involves something called "lesbian baiting," in which a male soldier will pressure a female soldier into either accepting his sexual advances or facing accusations of lesbianism. In other cases, lesbian baiting serves to keep a female officer from advancing in rank. No matter how unfounded, those accusations will hurt or ruin her career.

Simply removing the ban on gays would stop lesbian baiting, a practice that targets both gay and heterosexual female soldiers. It would also free gay soldiers from needing to make up lies about their lives in order to protect the policies of an institution that preaches honesty and integrity. Finally, it would also make it more difficult for anyone to blackmail gay soldiers with threats of outing, if coming out wouldn't hurt their careers. Obviously, unjust laws create atmospheres where further injustices can flourish.

Despite the phrasing of "Don't ask, don't tell," the policy still allows the removal of soldiers from active duty who get outed some other way, such as someone reporting them. Regardless of how the commanding officers learn, it usually leads to American soldiers—people willing to fight and die for their country—losing pensions, benefits, and livelihood. In many cases, they must pay back scholarships and other funds. A decorated soldier who fought in wars and also risked life and limb in emergency aid situations suddenly becomes a criminal, just because of sexual orientation.

With America's military stretched so thin, many soldiers facing extended tours, and many retired soldiers called back into active duty, I would think we could throw out such a ludicrous rule as saying openly gay people can't serve. Certainly, some people shouldn't serve, but I can't understand how being gay could justify turning someone away. If I had a son or daughter giving up day after day of life with family and safety, I would gladly say to a qualified, decent candidate, "Yes, please go over there and serve, so my child can come home sooner. Thank you!" Instead, we persecute many of our soldiers for society's prejudice.

# "SURVEYS PROVE GAYS ARE A MUCH SMALLER NUMBER THAN THEY CLAIM, THAT THEIR AVERAGE LIFESPAN IS 44 YEARS, AND THAT THEY HAVE 5000–15,000 PARTNERS PER YEAR."

Surveys prove nothing but how gullible people become when someone throws around numbers. Unfortunately, many people believe the old lie of "Statistics don't lie." From my observations, users of surveys often seem to choose from easy steps like the following:

(1) Only survey a few people, probably those on their misinformation mailing list or those visiting their misinformation Web sites, but then claim the documented views represent most Americans. Any survey of a few hundred people cannot possibly hint at the views of "most Americans," especially not if the people in the survey group all belong to the same organization, occupation, religious denomination, or political party.

(2) Include misinformation with the survey. For example, "If you support the anti-discrimination law, you will give gays special rights, so do you support the anti-discrimination law?" In some cases, the misinformation will take up a separate page or more, while the survey itself will use straightforward questions, so the surveyor can quote the questions without admitting to using misinformation. The misinformation still affected the answers.

(3) Use stats that apply to certain members of a group, but make it sound like they apply to the entire group. For example, take the findings from the gay male patients of an STD clinic in San Francisco and apply them to all gays, or take the income stats that apply to the gay male readers of a fashion magazine and apply them to all gays. Why not use the heterosexual male patients of an STD clinic or the heterosexual male readers of fashion magazines to represent all heterosexuals?

(4) Slant the survey questions and/or the available answers. This way, the person must give or seem to give an answer s/he would not usually give.

(5) Building on #4, use dense, obfuscated jargon, so the survey groups must answer questions they can't even understand. Politicians, lawyers, lobbyists, and insurance adjusters can write such surveys in their sleep. Frustrated and confused, the survey groups will eventually give a different answer than they would have given if they understood the language. We might call this one "the fine print approach."

(6) Use outdated and/or refuted stats, a favorite tactic on the religious and political programs of Sunday morning television.

(7) Ask personal questions with others present and/or one's social security number required, then make the results available to the survey group's employers, but call the survey anonymous. All employers have access to the social security numbers of their employees, and any resourceful person can find someone's identity from that person's social security number. A famous sex survey even allowed one's family members to remain present while the person answered the questions aloud, but the surveyors still called it "anonymous." How can anyone trust those answers?

(8) Use "most" in place of any number above 50 that suits their purpose. Thus, "52% of the Americans in the survey group favor the bill" becomes "most Americans favor the bill." Most Americans won't think about the fact that "most" can mean something much less than "almost everyone."

(9) Make up stats, and maybe even make up a source. Most people (meaning "almost everyone") won't bother checking.

Unfortunately, one example of these distortions came from some gay-friendly companies that wanted advertisers to target gays, but only succeeded in feeding the Religious Right the lie that all gays are rich, own homes, etc.; the RR turned around and asked why gays keep claiming discrimination when we're actually the so-called "gay elite." Of the myriad gays I've met, only a few are wealthy. Is there an office somewhere that sends gays a million dollars when they come out? If so, I need that office's phone number. Where's my check?

If we believe all statistics, then we must believe those used in *The Bell Curve*, a book that supposedly proves the intellectual superiority of whites over blacks. We should know not to trust statistics when one TV commercial says "9 out of 10 doctors give X pain reliever to their patients," but another commercial says "90% of doctors prefer Y pain reliever," and yet another says "surveys prove doctors recommend Z pain reliever more than any other."

We also hear many baked stats during political campaigns, with the opposite party offering opposite so-called "facts" from their surveys. The fact that surveys tend to contradict each other proves that we should stop seeing statistics as something written by the hand of God on Mt. Sinai. We should also pick up on the fact that the numbers "90%" and "9 out of 10" occur a little too often for credulity.

Many people argue against gay equality (including gay marriage) on the grounds that surveys show most Americans not supporting it, but surveys in the 1940s showed most Americans not supporting American intervention in the

Holocaust or America releasing its Japanese citizens from American detainment camps, while surveys in the 1960s showed most Americans not supporting racial desegregation or interracial marriage. Fortunately, we finally decided not to let those surveys think for us, regardless of their accuracy or inaccuracy.

But I want to look at the supposed accuracy of some of the statistics that the Religious Right uses against gays.

"Surveys prove there are just a few gays." Some deliberately slanted surveys falsely claim to prove gays only exist as one or two per cent of the population, which supposedly makes it all right to discriminate against us.

Keep in mind that (1) most gays live in denial at least part of their lives, and while in denial, they won't even acknowledge their gayness to themselves, much less to a survey; (2) at least one of those surveys only considered people gay if they not only identify themselves as gay but also have never had a single sexual encounter with a member of the opposite sex; (3) the same survey made contemporary America sound like the most sexually chaste society in the history of civilization—which should make everyone question the survey's veracity; (4) a lie with a number attached to it is still a lie; (5) except during the punishment phase of a murder trial, no one should debate other people's right to exist; (6) as long as we can justify discrimination against any minority group, we should consider everyone's freedom in danger and another Holocaust just a heartbeat away—as some countries continue to learn. Also keep in mind that the incredible gay presence on the internet suggests that our number is much higher than any research has ever shown.

As I clarified before, outnumbering the minority can't justify mistreating the minority. We are people, not statistics. Ultimately, it doesn't matter how many or how few of us exist…only that we are human beings.

Here's another one: "The average gay man won't live to be 44." I know as many gay men over 44 as under 44, but I keep hearing this ridiculous claim, which came from a carefully slanted study. It involved reading certain gay publications for the obituaries of certain gay men who went to certain gay bars—men who were young, openly gay, and living in big cities. The study completely ignored the facts that many gays are closeted, that many gays live in rural areas with no gay bars, and that most elderly people (gay or nongay) aren't exactly bar-hoppers. Yet, the study supposedly reflected all gays.

Even if those baked stats were true, would that mean we should discriminate against young black men because of their high death rate? Sometimes using 42, 43, or 45 as the number, so-called "family values" groups keep applying this statistic to all gay men or even to all homosexuals, though health-care workers denounce that misinformation. The fact that so many of these groups can't even repeat the lie accurately suggests that they probably never question the lie itself.

If any stat suits their purpose, they will elevate that stat to the same level as scripture—if not higher. Thus, they will see it as irrefutable. In quoting such stats, some otherwise honest people will make statements like the following: "That number came from some highly reliable research."

Videos like *The Gay Agenda* and *Gay Rights, Special Rights* use sham statistics and gay fringe groups to represent all gays. For example, they will show some gays into S&M (sadomasochism, sexual role-playing that usually involves leather and mild violence) then claim all gays like that; actually, some gays like S&M, just as some heterosexuals like it. Or they will mention an isolated group of gays throwing condoms at a priest, as a protest to AIDS apathy, and make that sound like all gays.

Considering the anti-gay rhetoric of heterosexual fringe groups, why not make Aryan Nations represent all heterosexuals? Why not make the business leaders who frequent topless bars represent all heterosexuals? Why not mention the fact that our supposedly puritanical counterparts manage to keep heterosexual erotica in the top 20 of movie sales/rentals charts most of the time? I couldn't care less if nongays want to buy erotica, but those charts prove that many nongays take great interest in sex for reasons other than reproduction. At least those videos never try to pass themselves off as holy.

Though mostly made by religious fundamentalists, anti-gay videos contain many made-up statistics and other lies. Why do some people who claim to stand for Truth with a capital "T" have so much trouble telling the truth with a small "t"? How can lies glorify God? Remember the list in Romans 1, the one people like to use against gays? It also says that God won't allow liars into Heaven.

Of course, family values groups will say anything to convince their supporters to send more money. Their tactic relies on (1) depicting gays as self-destructive monsters that want to destroy society, religion, marriage, the family, and America, then (2) claiming they can stop the so-called "homosexual agenda" through the generous financial donations of so-called "real Americans." Of course, they also imply that God will grant miracles to people who send them money.

Another approach of family values groups requires soliciting requests for advice; the advice supposedly comes from the group's founder, but he actually lets his employees tailor his form letters to fit the questions. His employees then put the advice seekers on a mailing list, to receive a barrage of anti-gay propaganda, sent out tax-free; not surprisingly, that propaganda usually includes a request for money. Though they portray gays as a privileged class, most televangelists live in luxury, thanks to the contributions they swindle from the elderly, the disabled, and the desperate.

Generally, other pastors work strictly on a local church level, making moderate salaries, if any at all; regardless of how their theological views might differ from mine and each other's, I see most of those pastors as essentially honest. However, people who belong to the national, TV/radio personality breed of pastor seem to value money more than honesty, justice, or even God. The same goes for those who use political office as a lucrative religious office.

They carefully manipulate and claim exclusive rights to terms like "family, Christian, values," etc. If anyone dares disagree with them, they cry "anti-family, anti-Christian, anti-values," when really the person was merely disagreeing with them. If I disagree with the way you cook pizza, does that make me anti-pizza? If I say I like pizza, does that automatically mean I like pizza cooked your way or that I only like your favorite toppings? I can disagree with you while still loving and valuing God, country, and family. I can care about traditional values without holding your traditional values. I can value the family without wanting to father children.

Anyone interested in a real family values group needs to look up the nearest chapter of PFLAG (Parents, Families, and Friends of Lesbians and Gays), an organization dedicated to keeping families together and helping those families secure equal rights for each other. They even allow their members to disagree with each other, to be different from each other, and (here comes the scary part) to think for themselves. Many of PFLAG's members joined too late, after losing their children to suicide, AIDS, hate crimes, or some other tragedy, but those members now work hard to encourage others not to wait until tragedy occurs.

We need to love each other unconditionally. Life offers too little time for us to waste any of it on conditional love. Why wait until someone's funeral to decide you needed to spend more time with that person?

Of course, gays have no spare time, if you believe this statistic: "The average gay male has 5000–15,000 different partners per year." The number varies within that range every time I hear or read it, and sometimes says "in his lifetime," instead of "per year." To make any version of the claim even physically possible, the average gay man must live in San Francisco or New York City and somehow remain both eighteen and unemployed his entire life. Either that, or all gay men are traveling salesmen.

Our numbers must exceed the percentages I mentioned above, if we can all find so many different partners. Say Bret lives in a town with a population of 3500 and fairly close to a town with a population of 6500. If only 2% of any given population is gay, but over half the population is female, how will he find 5000 gay men? You do the math. Even if 10% of the population is gay, that still leaves only about 5% as gay males.

In both those cases, we make the false assumptions that Bret somehow manages to identify every gay man, that he manages to get them all alone, that he finds them all attractive, and that they all find him attractive. Keep in mind that (1) no one's gaydar (gay radar) works all the time, (2) tastes differ, (3) even desperate men will turn down anyone who turns them off enough, (4) small-town gossip will keep closet cases away from Bret, (5) most gays in small towns are closet cases, and (6) most men decrease in virility after a certain age. Of course, new people are born into or move into Bret's area, but the life-span of one human being simply won't allow Bret to meet his gay sex quota of at least 5000–15,000 different partners over his lifetime, much less each year of his lifetime.

Will the gay police take away his so-called "special rights" and his supposed "gay elite" payments? Will Judge RuPaul ban him from beauty school, antiques shops, West Hollywood, and the *Oklahoma* auditions? Or will Bret somehow seduce thousands of heterosexual men before the gay IRS audits him?

A lot of men (gay or nongay) desire multiple partners, though most adulterous husbands (again, gay or nongay) go to great lengths to conceal their pre-marital and extra-marital encounters, putting their unsuspecting wives at risk of STD's. Because of this shared attitude among so much of the male population, it should surprise no one that many gay men see nothing wrong with promiscuity. It makes much less sense that so many heterosexual men find heterosexual promiscuity heroic for men but disgusting for women. On the other hand, many gay and nongay men consider promiscuity unattractive for everyone, or they may feel certain desires but decide it isn't worth the risk of betraying and hurting their loved ones.

According to medical statistics (not just surveys), STD's tend to spread quickly on college campuses because of certain male students finding so many different female partners but feigning exclusivity, often using the withdrawal method in place of a condom. Of course, many gay and nongay men will go through life with few partners, only one, or none at all. Some women also have multiple partners, either by choice or because their partners leave them.

When it comes to reliability, anti-gay statistics add up to one number: zero. Numbers shouldn't replace thinking.

# "Homosexuals are just a bunch of men dressing up like women."

Actually, some gay men dress in drag, for fun or profit. A gay man who, as the jargon goes, "does drag" might only assume his female persona when he plans to participate in a drag show, or he might also wear it for clubbing and parties. He probably won't wear it many other places.

In some movies, the gay characters are all wimpy men who do drag and live in drag, but people need to stop confusing movies with reality. Far from epitomizing the stereotype of gay men as wimps, many drag queens have been the most courageous and aggressive leaders of the gay equality movement, daring to come out, daring to demand equality, and daring to mock patriarchal oppression. Of course, many of them do drag for silly, exaggerated drama.

Some people experience a sort of quirk called "cross-dressing," which makes them want to occasionally dress as the opposite gender. Nongays with this desire will usually practice it privately, at home; it not only fulfills some need within them but also helps them identify with the other gender, an identifying that could strengthen heterosexual relationships. However, most heterosexual cross dressers must look a long time before finding an understanding spouse, and they should probably reveal their quirk to a potential spouse before marriage, to avoid the pain of a broken marriage. As these heterosexual cross dressers learn, American culture fears any blurring or re-evaluation of gender roles and human sexuality, though countless Americans will still overlook serious relationship problems like domestic violence or co-dependence.

Some people experience a need to cross-dress for biological reasons. Though many disagree with the meanings or usefulness of the following terms (and the myriad other terms that try to explain gender differences), it might help to note them. The terms "transgender" and "transsexual" are somewhat fluid, tending to change over time and according to the person using them; their complexity probably causes so much disagreement, but I will attempt to simplify them. The term "transgender" often (but not always) refers to various gender differences, including cross-dressing and the following. The term "transsexual" often (but not always) refers to a cross dresser who feels trapped inside the wrong gender, or to people who receive gender-altering surgery, because they feel they were born with or given the wrong genitalia. In some cases, these people had already spent much of their lives dressing as—and maybe even passing as—the gender with which they identify.

When children are born with mixed or indefinite genitalia, the doctors will sometimes make a penis if enough flesh is there, but they usually just make a vagina. Those surgeries happen constantly, often without the doctors asking or even notifying the parents. Obviously, that situation invites guesswork and mistakes. Why should we hate those who feel trapped with the wrong results? They had no choice in the matter. Fortunately, some doctors will at least consult the parents, and some parents even decide to hold off on the surgery until the child is old enough to choose. Some adults remain intersexed (hermaphroditic).

Of course, thinking of all gays as men in dresses reflects the patriarchal practice of disregarding women. We can also find lesbian drag or women who feel trapped in the wrong gender. We can find women who dress as men for psychological, social, business, or entertainment reasons.

For example, many women avoid wearing so-called "feminine" attire to work, because such clothing might decrease their chances of a promotion but increase their chances of sexual harassment. Thus, they wear clothing commonly seen as masculine or even gender neutral. Or they might find traditionally feminine clothes simply uncomfortable and constrictive. The ideas of properly female or properly male clothing relates mostly to fashion trends, marketing gimmicks, and tradition; still, society still deems those ideas as above reproach, especially for men. While I never plan to cross-dress, I certainly appreciate how cross dressers dare to question those ideas.

Gays owe drag queens a great deal. The gay pride movement suddenly became visible during the 1960s, when a group of drag queens at New York's Stonewall Inn decided to fight back against police raids and police brutality. Across the country, police officers would beat up and arrest people just for going to a bar with a largely gay clientele, and newspapers would then print the list of "perverts," causing those people to lose their jobs and/or contemplate suicide. That trend had occurred off and on for decades. The Stonewall uprising led to change. Those "wimpy" drag queens turned over some police cars, stopped the police raids, and added to the anti-discrimination movement that had already started brewing in San Francisco.

Not surprisingly, trans people are frequent targets of discrimination and hate crimes. Also not surprisingly, they are constantly misunderstood or rejected, even by certain gay people who suffer from internalized homophobia and fear that trans people might perpetuate stereotypes about gay people. Of course it's hard to understand people who defy our definitions of man or woman. In fact, many people with gender differences don't fit into the neat categories we create for them, and many of them resent attempts at labeling them. Many of them don't understand themselves. But, please, stop thinking that gay and trans always over-lap, or that you have the right to beat up, murder, harass, or discriminate against any group. I'd rather meet a seven-foot, hairy-chested man in a blouse than a hateful person any day.

# REACTIONS TO HOMOPHOBIA: CONCLUSION

As I countered anti-gay comments, I kept noticing two points: (1) they often focus on gay men, either ignoring lesbians, or attacking all women indirectly by showing femininity as something negative; (2) I formerly believed and internalized much of the homophobia I address here. This was my journey into changing the way I see others and myself, and into trying to help more people accept themselves and each other.

But what about that focus on gay men? When people simply say, "Homosexuals are at much higher risk for AIDS," they're lying. The truth is that gay men are at much higher risk than nongay men, while nongay women are at much higher risk than lesbians. If AIDS is supposed to convince men to refrain from gay sex, is it also supposed to convince women to refrain from heterosexual intercourse? If women want babies, they can always use the more sanitary approach of artificial insemination.

We need to stop ignoring the simple fact that lesbians exist—a fact that even gay men, gay organizations, and gay publications often fail to acknowledge. The terms "homosexual" and "gay" include lesbians; since women outnumber men in the general population, we can disregard surveys and assume that the terms "homosexual," "gay," "bisexual," and (to use a term I despise) "the gay lifestyle" refer to at least as many women as men. Homophobes also rely on lesbian invisibility when they tell the lie that all gays engage in penis-to-anus penetration. Many gay men restrict themselves to oral sex, masturbation, mutual masturbation, abstinence, or even heterosexual intercourse. At least some, if not many, heterosexuals engage in penis-to-anus intercourse; in fact, many self-identified virgins among the heterosexual population actually pretend oral sex and anal sex "don't count." As far as I know, lesbians have vaginas, not penises, so they cannot engage in penis-to-anus intercourse. (We won't discuss strap-on toys.)

Homophobic clichés often reveal that many people see women as not even human, not even worth mentioning, and certainly not even capable of manifesting a sexual orientation. Do nongay women really want to protect such misogynist attitudes? Do they really want men to keep seeing all things feminine as inferior, negligible, and best kept quiet? Do they really not notice when religious fundamentalists use "feminization" as a dirty word and refer to it as a threat to America?

No wonder so many nongay women support gay equality and say they love their gay male friends; gay men often treat women better than nongay men treat women. We need nongay women as allies, and they need us to help expose the lingering misogyny in society.

We all need to address sexism. Why do homophobic lies tend to exclude gay women? Why not mention the committed relationships or low HIV rates of lesbians? What makes so many heterosexual men get off on lesbian fantasies but see gay men as a threat? Why can't lesbians pose a threat? Why not make "Alice and Eve" remarks as readily as the tired "Adam and Steve" remark? Should we look at the connections between homophobia and other insecurities, such as the fear that women will destroy the gap between male and female job opportunities, the fear that one's wife will see herself as more than merely a walking womb, or the fear that society can survive without male domination?

Homophobia always comes back to the meaning of its last three syllables: fear or hatred. Fear and hatred distort our thinking and our interactions. The climate of fear and hatred even causes gay people to hate themselves, making them more likely to risk or even take their lives.

Ultimately, I wrote this essay not for hard-core bigots but for any nongays who will listen, for any gays who want to stop hating themselves, for anyone who feels a need to take a stand against injustice, and for helping in my own battle against internalized homophobia. I think most people who make homophobic remarks are merely misinformed, so we need to reach them with accurate information and real-life examples, even if reaching them means coming out as gay or as the family members of a gay person.

We can reach a lot of the merely misinformed people; only God can reach the KKK, Aryan Nations, Christian Identity, Concerned Women of America, etc. For fear of more suicides and suicidal behavior, we desperately need to reach the closet cases and denial cases that believe and sometimes even repeat the terrible lies they hear about themselves. I offer my concluding comments for any LGBTs who, like my former self, might internalize homophobia.

Treat other people's insecurities as their weakness, not as a reason to hate yourself or remain silent. Try to inform others and get along with others, but never base self-acceptance on whether others accept you. Hateful knee-jerk phrases can stick in your mind, like a worn-out song you never liked in the first place, but you should learn to see yourself as beautiful and wonderful. If others fail to see you that way, consider it their loss.

Accept yourself, and take action. We can move past the "Reactions to Homophobia" now. After you finish reading *Holding Me Together*, find a copy of *50 Ways to Support Lesbian and Gay Equality: The Complete Guide to Supporting Family, Friends, Neighbors or Yourself*. That wonderful book offers pro-active ways to change the world for the better. You can make a difference in your life, and in the lives of other LGBT people and their families. Refuse victim status, and use the voice that others try to deny you. Please also rely on the other resources that I include below; the same list appears with links on the "Reactions to Homophobia" page of DuaneSimolke.Com, which will also feature occasional updates.

Thanks for reading this extensive essay; please keep reading.

# REACTIONS TO HOMOPHOBIA: RESOURCES

Al-Fatiha Foundation. http://www.al-fatiha.org

AMERICAblog. http://www.americablog.org/

Besen, Wayne R. *Anything but Straight: Unmasking the Scandals and Lies Behind the Ex-Gay Myth*. Binghamton, NY: Harrington Park Press, 2003.

The Advocate; 6922 Hollywood Boulevard; Suite 1000; Los Angeles CA 90028. http://www.advocate.com

American Psychological Association. *Answers to Your Questions About Sexual Orientation and Homosexuality*. APA; 750 First Street, NE; Washington, DC 20002-4242. http://www.apa.org/

Amnesty International. *Breaking The Silence: Human Rights Violations Based On Sexual Orientation*. Amnesty International Publications; 322 Eighth Avenue; New York, NY 10001. http://www.amnesty.org/

Biblical Errancy. http://members.aol.com/ckbloomfld/

Blumenfeld, Warren J. (editor). *Homophobia: How We All Pay the Price*. Boston: Beacon Press, 1992.

Broderick, Greg R. "Dr. Paul Cameron and the Family Research Institute." The Radical Religious Right Pages.
http://www.qrd.org/QRD/www/RRR/cameron.html

Campaign to End Homophobia; P.O. Box 382401; Cambridge, MA 02238-2401. http://www.endhomophobia.org/

Capital Xtra; 251 Bank Street; Suite 503; Ottawa, Ontario K2P 1X3; Canada. http://www.xtra.ca/

Children Of Lesbians And Gays Everywhere. Colage; 3543 18th ST #17; San Francisco, CA 94110. http://www.colage.org

Christians Against Bible Abuse (CABA).
http://www.christians-against-bibleabuse.us/

Day, David. *Things They Never Told You In Sunday School: A Primer For The Christian Homosexual.* S. Norwalk, CT: Lavender, 1987.

Delta Lambda Phi National Social Fraternity; 1008 Tenth Street, Suite 374; Sacramento, CA 95814. http://www.dlp.org/

Equality for Gays and Lesbians Everywhere (Egale). Egale Canada; 310–396 Cooper St.; Ottawa, ON, K2P 2H7. http://www.egale.ca/

Equal Partners in Faith; 2026 P Street NW; Washington, DC 20036.
http://www.geocities.com/CapitolHill/4497/EqualPartners.html

Ex-ex-gays. URL no longer active. Please see these related pages:
http://members.aol.com/exgaynomad/,
http://www.exgaywatch.com/xgw/2003/10/christian_exexg.html,
http://www.publiceye.org/equality/x-gay/X-Gay-10.html

Fahy, Una. *How To Make The World A Better Place For Gays And Lesbians.* New York: Warner, 1995.

Family Pride; P.O. Box 34337; San Diego, CA 92163.
http://www.familypride.org/

Federal Bureau of Investigation; J. Edgar Hoover Building; 935 Pennsylvania Avenue, NW; Washington, D.C. 20535-0001.
http://www.fbi.gov/

Fone, Byrne. *Homophobia: A History.* New York: Picador, 2000.

Gomes, Peter J. *The Good Book: Reading the Bible with Mind and Heart.* New York: Morrow, 1996.

Gay and Lesbian Alliance Against Defamation (GLAAD).
http://www.glaad.org/

Gay/Lesbian/Straight Educators Network. GLSEN; 121 West 27th Street; Suite 804; New York, NY 10001. http://www.glsen.org/

HateCrime.org. http://hatecrime.org/

Helminiak, Daniel A. *What the Bible Really Says About Homosexuality*. New Mexico: Alamo Square, 2000.

Holy Bible. Prefer the *King James Version*, *New International Version*, or *Revised Standard Version*, as the others are less reliable.

Homosexuals: Victims of the Nazi Era.
http://www.holocaust-trc.org/homosx.htm

Interfaith Working Group; PO Box 11706; Philadelphia, PA 19101.
http://www.iwgonline.org/

Janoff, Douglas Victor. *Pink Blood: Homophobic Violence in Canada*. Toronto: University of Toronto Press, 2005. http://www.pinkblood.ca/

Jim Bilbrey's Care Page. http://www.geocities.com/WestHollywood/4254/

Kader, Rev. Samuel. *Openly Gay Openly Christian: How the Bible Really is Gay Friendly*. San Francisco: Leyland, 1999.

Koskovich, Gerard. "The Nazi Persecution of Homosexuals: An Annotated Bibliography of Nonfiction Sources in English."
http://members.aol.com/dalembert/lgbt_history/nazi_biblio.html

Lambda 10 Project for GLB Greeks. Indiana University; 705 East Seventh Street; Bloomington, IN 47405. http://www.lambda10.org/

Lautmann, Ruediger. "Gay Prisoners in Concentration Camps as Compared with Jehovah's Witnesses and Political Prisoners."
http://www.mtsu.edu/~baustin/lautmann.html

Lesbian/Gay Rights Lobby of Texas. LGRL; P.O. Box 2340; Austin, TX 78768. http://www.lgrl.org/

Log Cabin Republicans; National Office; 1633 Q St., NW #210; Washington, DC 20009. http://www.lcr.org/

Maran, Meredith, with Angela Watrous (editors). *50 Ways to Support Lesbian and Gay Equality: The Complete Guide to Supporting Family, Friends, Neighbors or Yourself.* Maui: Inner Ocean Publishing, 2005.

Marcus, Eric. *Is It A Choice? Answers To 300 of the Most Frequently Asked Questions About Lesbians and Gays.* San Francisco: Harper, 1999.

Metropolitan Community Churches (MCC). http://www.mccchurch.org

Mohr, Richard. *The Long Arc of Justice: Lesbian and Gay Marriage, Equality, and Rights.* New York: Columbia University Press, 2005.

National Gay and Lesbian Task Force Foundation (the Task Force). 1325 Massachusetts Ave NW, Suite 600, Washington, DC 20005. http://www.thetaskforce.org/

The National Museum & Archive of Lesbian And Gay History. *The Gay Almanac.* New York: Berkley, 1996.

"New Study Links Homophobia with Homosexual Arousal." Excerpted from "Is Homophobia Associated With Homosexual Arousal?" by Henry E. Adams, Ph.D., Lester W. Wright, Jr., Ph.D. and Bethany A. Lohr, University of Georgia, in Journal of Abnormal Psychology, Vol. 105, No. 3.

okgay. http://okgay.tripod.com/

Out; 110 Green Street; Suite 600; New York, NY 10012. http://out.com

Parents, Families, and Friends of Lesbians and Gays. PFLAG; 1101 14th St.; N.W., Suite 1030; Washington, DC 20005. http://www.pflag.org/

Penman, Alexander. *Beyond Religion.* (See his Web site for details.) http://www.geocities.com/Athens/Cyprus/7128/

People For the American Way; 2000 M Street, NW, Suite 400; Washington, DC 20036. http://www.pfaw.org/

People With A History. http://www.fordham.edu/halsall/pwh/index.html

Reconciling Congregations Program; 3801 N. Keeler Avenue; Chicago, IL 60641. http://www.rcp.org/

Religious Tolerance. "Religious Groups' Policies Towards Homosexuals And Homosexuality." http://www.religioustolerance.org/hom_chur.htm

Rutledge, Leigh W. *The New Gay Book of Lists*. Los Angeles: Alyson, 1996.

Scroggs, Robin. *The New Testament and Homosexuality*. Philadelphia: Fortress, 1983.

Sears, James T. Rebels, *Rubyfruit, and Rhinestones: Queering Space in the Stonewall South*. New Brunswick: Rutgers University Press, 2001.

Sexual Orientation: Science, Education, and Policy. http://psychology.ucdavis.edu/rainbow/index.html

Shilts, Randy. *Conduct Unbecoming: Gays & Lesbians in the Military*. New York: St. Martin's, 1993.

Spong, John Shelby. *Living In Sin? A Bishop Rethinks Human Sexuality*. San Francisco: Harper, 1988.

Straight Spouse Network. SSN; 8215 Terrace Drive; El Cerrito, CA 94530-3058. http://www.ssnetwk.org

Sullivan, Andrew. Partners Task Force for Gay & Lesbian Couples. Buddy-buddy; Box 9685; Seattle, WA 98109-0685. http://www.buddybuddy.com/

towleroad. http://towleroad.typepad.com/towleroad/

Y Forum on People's Differences. http://www.yforum.com/index.html

# Part Two:
# Poems and Short Essays

# HOME

When I lie beside him,
His knee presses
Against the underside
Of my knee,
His hand presses
Against my chest,
As if holding me together.
If I wake,
And he isn't beside me,
I'll curl up
Like a frightened child,
Lost in the dark,
Afraid to move.
If I wake,
And he isn't beside me,
The thickest blanket
Won't keep me warm
But I wake,
And find him
Beside me.
He holds me together.

# CHASING SEAGULLS

After a vacation that went too long,
An excursion for you,
Me, and your best friend Janice,
You kept trying to convince me
To stay with you in New Orleans.
Always another decoy,
Or acting like a bird
With broken wings,
Supposedly stuck in the French Quarter,
More by injury
Than by desire.

You couldn't look wounded;
I couldn't look away.
Janice went home first.
She said "Don't worry,"
To us, to herself.
She left New Orleans,
Calling it Jericho,
Hearing trumpets, avoiding walls.
Her kitten feet tested the airport escalator.

Alone, a couple,
We danced on loading docks,
Took pictures of seagulls,
Fell into the water,
Hoping to float like driftwood.

I designed your Mardi Gras mask.
We wore the Mardi Gras beads
That we swung at each other
As if scaring away evil spirits.
Now I leave New Orleans, and you promise
My mailbox will smell like salt air
From your letters.

# RAINBOW

The little boy
Leans over the counter,
Dollar bill in hand.
Asking if they carry other flavors.

The clerk's eyes narrow as he says,
"We only carry vanilla."
The clerk waves his hand
Across the ten open barrels
Of white ice cream.
"Other colors suggest…
A certain agenda.
White suggests traditional values."

The boy goes from almost crying
To almost laughing.
"Why should it matter
Which flavor I like?
Besides, I can't make myself
Like a certain flavor,
Even if everyone else likes it."

The clerk crosses his arms.
"Maybe I could sell you
Some chocolate syrup.
Don't put it on the ice cream
Until you sneak away somewhere."

Laughing,
The little boy crumples his dollar
Back into his pocket
And leaves.

# HOW "CHILDREN IN THE STREETS" WROTE ITSELF

The poem "Children in the Streets" began when I saw a brief report on the ABC news about South American children left homeless and parentless by constant fighting. The children huddled together, in groups of over a dozen. Still in my teens, it struck me how much more comfortably I lived than children in so many other places.

I wanted to write about these children, but not until I found the most effective words. Several weeks later, at a Gibson's department store, I saw the cover of U2's album *War*. U2, still an obscure band at that time, had gained my interest when I first heard their song "New Year's Day," which expressed the anti-war sentiments they gained from growing up in war-torn Ireland. The cover of U2's album displayed the word "WAR" in blood-red capital letters, with a black and white picture. Instead of showing soldiers fighting, the picture showed a hungry child, with a cut lip, and with a wounded stare that ripped into my soul.

The next day, I read an issue of *Reader's Digest* while in the waiting room of a doctor's office. On a page dedicated to vocabulary improvement, I saw the word "ire," defined as "a cold, hateful stare." "Ire" struck me as the perfect word for the boy on the album cover and the children in the news story. They stared with a hatred unlike that of the warring factions. Rather than hating some designated enemy, they hated the senselessness of someone taking their families, shelter, safety, and innocence. They hated violence.

I first wrote "Children in the Streets" as a song poem in 1983. Composers would say they loved it, but none of them could produce what they considered the right melody for it. Frustrated that, after more than a decade, no one ever heard "Children in the Streets," I decided people should read it. In 1995, I wrote the following free verse version; the song version appears after that.

# CHILDREN IN THE STREETS

Six years old,
He watches his home burn,
Watches the soldiers run.

As he eyes them with cold ire,
He no longer wants answers;
He only wants to escape
The games with guns.

His father and brother
Went to "revolution."
Once people go there,
They never return.

That was his mother's way
Of saying they died,
Just like everyone else.
Just like she soon died.

Someone else's fathers
And brothers
Came for "revolution,"
Came for "show of power."

The boy meets up
With other lost children;
They stay together,
Having no one else.

Their parents always said
"Be good or be punished,"
So they wonder what they did
To receive this punishment.

They wonder about words:
Revolution, power, punish.

They wander through rubble:
Revolution, power, punish.

# CHILDREN IN THE STREETS (SONG VERSION)

Six years old
He watched his home turn into fire
As the soldiers ran
He eyed them with cold ire
He doesn't want an answer
He just wants to escape
This strange game with guns
That's gotten worse of late

His father won't be back
He went to revolution
He said a show of power
Is our people's only solution
The soldiers are like his father
They do what they're told
But in the rubble
Who reaps what they sow?

Children in the streets
Who are they? No one cares to know
They live in the streets
Because they have nowhere else to go

He meets up with others
So much like himself
They will stay together
Since they have no one else
Why are they condemned?
They've done nothing wrong
They just pray for the day
The soldiers will be gone

Children in the streets
Who are they? No one cares to know
They live in the streets
Because they have nowhere else to go

Revolution, power, progress

Peace on earth
Now we must demand
Please don't turn away
Please try to understand
They're paying for the things
We never should have done
If we're so advanced
Why can't we live as one?

# FRIDAY AFTERNOON SPECTRUM

Mountains collide,
Splashing diamond slivers,
Shattering office windows,
Sending glass and diamonds
Over the warriors at the board meeting.

Warriors reach into carpet,
Try to find diamonds in glass,
Cut their hands.

Warriors wield prize belts,
Scream about their titles,
Wield atomic power packs,
Return to outer space.

# RECEPTION

I based this poem
On a soap opera scene
Which someone based on a romance novel,
Which someone based on a song,
Which someone based on a true story,
As told in the tabloids.
I know it's real.
It's really all I know.

4 AM:
What will the gods create
From the chaos
On my TV screen?
Something will happen soon.

# ALBUM

I could never mention your lisp
without revealing mine.
Still hoping to sound wise,
I said if you buy an old house,
inspect it for termites.
If you buy a new house,
think of it as a setting
for 21st-century literature.

We could never walk through
the downtown cinema
without walking out our shoes.
We joked our way through
college and summer jobs
without worry of loans
or mortgages or if we
really loved each other.

I guess we didn't.
You met someone else.
Between our embraces?
Between our notes?
Between classes?
You never said;
I couldn't stand to ask.

You introduced me to him,
said we should
try to get our college crowd
back together after graduation.

The last time I saw you,
I knew I could let you go
and he would catch you.

That weekend
in the Smoky Mountains,
you laughed as if
you had never allowed yourself
to laugh before.

# CAN GOD CURE YOU?

(Author's note: At one point, I had merged this personal essay with one of the sections in my long essay "Reactions to Homophobia." It appeared that way in the first edition of *Holding Me Together*, but I later decided it didn't really fit the format of that section. It really speaks directly to gays, rather than to the people who want to "fix" us.)

One morning, I visited a Sunday school class where, to my discomfort, someone brought up the subject of gays. One of the people there made the following comments: "We should invite them into our church. After we read the Bible to them, they'd know they was wrong, and quit being gay."

Because of my closet status, I suppressed the emotions that rushed through my body. Besides, I couldn't decide whether to yell John 3:16, hand out PFLAG literature, crack up laughing, or just correct her dreadful grammar.

Still, she meant it. She believed it.

I can't believe it. Not after reading the Bible all the way through several times; after attending Baptist colleges for six and a half years; after surrounding myself with religious books, music, and movies; after taking part in homophobic rhetoric; or even after praying day after guilt-ridden day for God to make me what I saw as "normal." "Normal" meant accepted, and I yearned for acceptance. After all of that, I remained gay. Abstinent, but gay.

Still, the question remains for gays, can God cure you? Yes, God can cure you of the internalized homophobia that enters your mind through churches, schools, politicians, etc. God can cure you of self-hatred. God can make you a better person, one who sees sexuality as an important and beautiful part of one's uniqueness. God can use your differences as a way of teaching you tolerance, compassion, and respect for people who differ from the norm by race, disability, culture, religion, or other ways.

Countless gays have found peace with themselves and with God, by living honestly and openly as gays. God's love ignores the stop signs put up by those who hate you. God's love never requires the approval or permission of any church, politician, or group. Your love for yourself shouldn't require their approval or permission either.

# DIGGING UP "THE GARDENER"

When I wrote this next poem, I was a student at Belmont College (now Belmont University), in Nashville, Tennessee. Belmont's campus holds historical importance in Tennessee, especially the Belmont Mansion. Also, many people claim the mansion is haunted.

During my years at Belmont, I often heard stories about someone seeing a ghostly vision of a woman, descending the stairs in the mansion. The college newspaper even published a picture of a glowing object descending the stairs. It could have been a glare, or something on the lens, but folks on campus enjoyed talking about that mysterious blur!

A security guard once told me that he and another guard were walking through the mansion one night when they suddenly felt cold. Then they felt a presence, and could even feel that presence touching them!

Besides history and folklore, Belmont's campus is also popular because of its beautiful flowers. Flowers and a haunted mansion. That combination struck me one day.

I was sitting outside, supposedly finishing my homework. Gazing at the mansion, I wrote the first draft of the following poem. Good thing I had a pen and paper handy!

# THE GARDENER

The wind blows colder now.
Did I dangle myself on a string
that would soon become my noose?
Did I lock myself
in the vault I robbed?

As I tend gardens around
this mansion like my former home,
I seek the shadow
of its Victorian columns.
Still, I feel the cold,
as if the mansion itself produces
chills, fear, a presence.

I hear someone laugh
as the new owner escapes to his job.
But he lives alone,
and that phantom
gliding past the window,
ruffling the curtains,
lacks substance.
It doesn't seem real enough
to laugh.

The mansion is laughing,
knowing the owner might become
someone else's gardener.

## second year

sometimes he seems to wonder
why i see him
as more than he sees
why i settle with him
but he could just as easily
wonder why a rainbow
settles with colors

sometimes i wonder
if i can make him smile
like he makes me smile
as i lean into his arms
and feel the embrace
i wanted all my life

even if he cannot see
himself as i see him

a man who calls others
to ask if they
need him to listen
a man who tries to help

i could stand beside
anyone else
and still feel alone
as if in another country
a crowded country
where i understand
no words
no language
though everyone keeps
shouting at me

as if i should understand
as if i only pretend
not to understand

i want to hear his voice
i want to settle into
the embrace i wanted
all my life

# SEPARATED

I know the comfort of waves.
I hear the ocean calling
And count its salty echoes
As I stand on the cold shore.
You stand, watching from the cliff
And think I am a statue.

You never bother calling
Over the song of the waves
That bring their dance to the shore,
The pounding drums still echo.
What can disrupt a statue?
I never turn to the cliff.

I never stand on the cliff.
Why should I fear the calling?
Why should I not feel these waves?
Not feel the wind on the shore?
Not hear the chant of echoes?
Does that make me your statue?

I listen for a calling
As you cry upon your cliff
And curse my days on the shore.
Your screaming fades into waves;
You become a statue.
You only have its echoes.

Those are the frozen echoes;
That is your spirit calling.
That is what sculpted the cliff.
That is what allows the shore
To join the song of the waves,
Waking the human statue.

I never feel you calling.
I never hear those echoes.
I place myself on the shore.
You place yourself on the cliff.
The world becomes a statue.
We lose ourselves in the waves.

Searching between cliff and shore,
The statues will keep calling
Through the echoes of the waves.

# ANGELS AND RAZORS

We keep every room
As neat as possible:
Each a separate,
Well-ordered galaxy
In the universe of our home.

But every home
Has its refuse heap,
Its black hole,
Its corner for wreckage.

At first,
We used the spare bedroom
As a showcase for antiques.
Then we pushed boxes,
And whatever else would fit,
Under the bed.

Then scattered debris
Landed in the room:
Dry-flower arrangements,
Broken appliances,
Rechargeable razors…
Even the angel collection
That found no space
In our already crowded
Curio cabinet.

Two porcelain angels
Kneel between
Two rechargeable razors.
Forever graceful,
Forever innocent,
Forever well groomed.

# QUESTION

If I knock you down,
Kick you in the face,
No one will care.

The police, the newspaper,
The TV stations, the politicians
Will protect me
With their silence.
They will endorse me
With their closed eyes.

So I know I can
Rob you, beat you,
Make you bleed.

If you die, I can just say
"He smiled at me;
He smirked at me;
He disgusted me;
Because of my faith,
I find the homosexual lifestyle
Abhorrent;
Just read Leviticus."

So I will strike
With all my hatred,
All my fear,
Lashing out against
The you in me.

So I can go on
To my next victim,
So I can continue lurking
Outside your meeting places.

Because you fear leaving
The safety of the closet,
And because you hate
Yourself
Over the same differences
I hate,
You will never speak out,

Or will you?

# FACES, PART I

No one speaks at the funeral.
Jessica thinks of the phrase,
"Silence equals death."
The newspaper editor
Refused to print
What killed her daughter.
The obituary says, "Died
Of complications," instead of
"Died of AIDS complications."
Complications. How else
Could a thirty-year-old
Go from perfect health
To little more than a skeleton
With purple blotches on her skin?
Complications. Why else
Would a shy girl like Treena
Speak to churches and schools
About a disease
No one wants to mention?
Complications. Why else
Would the polyester preacher
And his flock
Circle the funeral like vultures
With signs that say
"God hates fags"
And "Thank God for AIDS"?
No one hated Treena
Until her husband's seed
Planted death in her blood.
Treena's mother can't understand
The silence, the signs,
The complications.
She can't understand
Why they call Treena gay
Or how that would justify
The march, the invasion.

She only understands
That her only child died.

# FACES, PART II

As Jessica holds the pale hand
Of the teenage boy,
She thinks of her daughter.
Like this forgotten child
Lying on his deathbed,
Treena contracted the virus
That causes silence.
Jessica's neighbors stopped visiting.
When she returned to work
After Treena's death,
Jessica's boss apologized,
Saying he had filled the vacancy.
Vacancy: an empty space,
A room
With something missing.
Now Jessica volunteers
At the AIDS hospice,
Trying to fill…vacancies.
The boy, Joey, says his parents
Won't visit him, or call him.
They said those who get AIDS
Deserve to die.
A vacancy, a child
Without parents to hold his hand.
He smiles and says
He remembers Treena,
The one who would speak about
The whispered word. A vacancy,
Passed from daughter to mother.

# FACES, PART III

I try not to see faces.
I want them to remain
Invisible, like the virus
I write about in my letters,
When asking for money.
Let me save you
From this curse,
From this plague
That they caused,
That they want to give you,
That they want to
Make you pay for,
That they want to use
As a way of making you cry,
Of making you
One of them.

# FACES, PART IV

Can you see yourself
In the disease
You blame on its victims?
It looks for a place to enter,
A wound, an opening.
It multiplies and spreads.
It preys without ceasing.
It never cares who it hurts,
As long as it gets what it wants.

# FACES, PART V

Adam sets a flower
On his wife's grave,
A white rose, every Sunday.
She died of cancer, the disease
Of warriors on white horses,
Not the disease of those
Whose funerals he pickets.
Still, sometimes lately,
He imagines someone
Blaming cancer, violence, divorce,
Floods, and earthquakes on her.
He imagines someone like himself
Looking for an enemy:
Not the devil—a human monster.
He ignores most of the activists
Until he finds one in leather or drag,
Until he hears of one
Throwing condoms at priests.
This one becomes the monster;
This one becomes them all.
A hand touches his shoulder.
He stands and turns around
To see the woman who ran crying
When he picketed the funeral
Of her daughter—one of them.
"You lost someone you loved,
Didn't you?" she asks,
And he nods.
She reaches into her purse
And takes out a picture
Of a smiling young woman
In a wedding gown.
"This is my daughter.
This is someone I loved.
She has a face."

# FACES, PART VI

At the funeral of a man
Who supported AIDS education,
Adam carries a sign
That says, "Fag Lover!"
The man's face, covered by oak,
Cannot scream back.
When Adam's wife died,
He couldn't stand to look
Into the casket, at her wax face;
She no longer looked real.
He always tries not to see
The face in the coffin.
But he keeps seeing the face
Of Jessica, and the picture
Of her daughter's face.
Unable to escape their faces,
He throws down the sign
And runs away.

# FACES, PART VII

At the hospice,
Jessica finds a white rose
With only her name on the card
Attached to its thorn-less stem.
Thinking she received it by mistake,
She gives it to Joey,
One of the many faces
No one wants to see.
Joey smiles, and holds her hand.
Vacancy: an empty space,
A room
With something missing.

# PROCESS

I wanted to know,
I asked,
If I could fashion a page,
Fashion a poem.
I wanted to read it to you
And see life breathed into sand.

My pen becomes
Doorways. Windows and eyes
Open, filling empty spaces,
Empty pages,
Until I see writing and living
As a single color,
Until I see your lips read my words
Through the years,
As eyes turn like hands of a clock.
Roads turn and spin webs
Around mountains
During your time
As my muse.

I want to write
Within storms,
To tear my poem from the stone
Of any language,
Of any etymology,
For someone listening
In any classroom.

I keep looking back over
An unpublished manuscript,
Never completed,
Still demanding a phrase,
As if one phrase can complete,
As if a thousand phrases can.

I pray; I sleep;
I wake to write you a poem.

# SONGS IN SIGN LANGUAGE

With hymns in hands,
You address us,
The deaf members
Of the congregation.

We cannot consume
All the sounds of the choir,
Though some of us
Hear certain notes.

Your lips move,
But I hear no sound,
As if you sing to us
From behind a window.

What makes your hands
Get caught in the stars,
The brook, and the breeze?
What makes you want
To sign these words to us?

Hands move,
Fingers twirling,
Waving.
Fists close,
Touch your heart,
Then open
And reach outward.

Keep your hands still
If you need to rest.
Your smile interprets
Every word of every song.

# FORGOTTEN

No one went in through the door;
no one went out,
as if it only stood
because someone built it.
We doubt its worth,
but how could we know?

No one looked in through the window;
no one looked out.
The blinds received strict orders
to admit no sunlight.
we sit at the table,
drink the coffee,
complain.

# SOCK POEM

(Author's note: I thought this poem was completely original when I wrote it, in response to an obvious situation. However, I later saw Jerry Seinfeld deliver a similar skit on TV, during a stand-up comedy special. Oh well…so many strange minds, so few subjects.)

I am like the sock I found
Early this morning
While running late for work.
After learning it sags a bit,
I learned it lacks a mate.

So I stuffed it into the back
Of the sock drawer,
The dark corner of the party
Where socks without mates
Converge but match no one.
Mates disappear
In hungry dryers,
Or during trips.

I throw away mates
Because of stains or tears.
But I could never throw away
A perfectly good sock.
I always assume I'll buy a pair
Exactly like the old pair.
Then the useless sock
Will become a back-up sock.

But it only joins
The growing, entangled mound
I must dig through several times
To find a perfect match.

I sometimes look for
A description in the personal ads:
"Single white sock seeks same."

Sometimes, when I run late,
Forget to compare
Color, length, stitching,
I grant my socks blind dates,
Interracial flings,
A chance to prove
Opposites attract.

But during lunch break,
I catch the offenders,
Fling them back into exile,
Telling myself
I should throw them away.

# HIGHER EDUCATION

Reach beyond
old school
hallways

that wind
and taper

into barren
courtyards.


# HAIKU

Outside my window,
The final leaves vanishing
With the autumn winds.


# TV SENYRU

(Author's note: according to knowledgerush.com, "Senryu is a Japanese form of
poetry similar to haiku in construction: three lines with a syllable pattern of 5-7-
5. However senryu tend to be about human foibles while haiku tend to be about
nature. Senryu do not need to include a season word like haiku. Much modern
haiku is more similar to senryu than traditional haiku.")

Now inside my brain,
A satellite receiver,
Two hundred channels!

# NOT WORTH DYING OVER

We sometimes hear that "The only safe sex is no sex." That sounds logical, but fails to allow for the sex drive. It also fails to allow for the mystique our taboo-oriented society gives sex, which makes it more appealing, secretive, and dangerous. Furthermore, adults in love with each other simply want to express their feelings by making love.

Sometimes, when sexually active people try to reconcile all those complications, they create some scary reasoning: "The only safe sex is no sex, so if I have sex, why bother with precautions?" We could also say "The only safe driving is no driving, so if I drive, why bother with traffic laws?" Why? Because disregarding them multiples the chances of the driver dying, or killing someone else.

Yes, many people became HIV positive through blood transfusions, rape, unfaithful partners, or a number of other ways. They had no choice. But countless other people simply choose to disregard safe sex, and some people even advertise their desire to engage in unprotected anal sex. Others go so far as to say they want the supposed "gift" of HIV, though most people who must endure HIV medications and the side-effects of those medications probably can't see it as a gift.

But, if you're not a heterosexual, maybe you deserve to die. Some people keep saying that. They make you feel ashamed of your sexual orientation. They think God will punish you for your differences from them, as if God made everyone in their image. Why validate their shallowness and hatred by destroying yourself? Homophobes love to see us kill ourselves, if not through suicide, then through suicidal, unprotected sex. It saves them all the effort of fire-bombings, gay-bashings, and anti-gay legislation.

In their minds, our illness or death somehow proves the righteousness of their hate agenda. They refer to us as trash, threats, and perverts; trick us into thinking God hates us; create laws that single us out for special discrimination; tell potentially violent people we pose a threat to them; and convince our parents that they should reject us.

Maybe you think you deserve all that abuse. Maybe, instead of reckless sex, you want to kill yourself by more expedient means, to escape the hatred and self-hatred. All the popular suicide methods tend to fail, often leaving the victim a mental or physical invalid, making life even more difficult. And if you succeed in your suicide attempt, it still leads to problems for all the loved ones you leave behind. Your lover, best friend, or younger relative might follow your example; after all, suicides tend to happen in cycles. Think about all the people you hurt.

Some terminally ill patients might build a case for suicide, but can emotional pain justify taking a human life?

By killing yourself, intentionally or through unsafe sex, you call yourself worthless and expendable. How can you think of a human being that way? Quit punishing yourself for the bigotry in society. Refuse to help the cause of homophobia. Take care of yourself. Learn to love yourself and protect yourself. See yourself and your partner as worth protecting. Treat safer sex as an act of defiance and gay pride, a statement about your love for yourself, a statement about the value of your life. Treat living each day as a tear in the fabric of bigotry.

Instead of seeing anti-gay discrimination as an excuse to hate yourself, see it as a call to protect human rights, to actively seek equality and justice for everyone. Check local and national gay publications—as well as the internet—to find ways to make a difference for yourself and all other people who fall outside the mainstream or the accepted.

Begin your stand by refusing to help those who want to destroy you. Dare to live a full, rich, happy life. It will annoy your accusers, while inspiring anyone else who faces your struggles.

# SIBLINGS, TEN VOICES

## I

My grandfather
wasn't born here
on this reservation.

We never wanted land
that we saw as ours,
or buildings
that trapped us inside,
or reservations
that reserved us
for poverty
and too much drink.

But those who come here
to gamble
should see our culture.
It still exists.
We still exist.

Grandfather told stories
of the buffalo
and the Great Spirit.
He passed down those stories
to me.

I can tell you
many stories, my son,
and help you learn from
the animals and the gods,
help you keep alive
that which makes us
us.

They put grandfather
on this reservation.
When he refused
to stay,
they refused
to let him
keep breathing the air
of the Western Plains,
or any other air.

He died for not wanting
to live in this cage
we call home.

## II

My father
thinks I care about stories
and buffalo.
My best friend died
of a drug overdose.

He was sixteen.

Can hearing about foxes,
bears, and snakes
bring him back?
Can turtles pay my college tuition,
or help me leave this place
that keeps calling me back?

I want nothing of his past,
because I want a future.
Why does he think
hearing about my great-grandfather's death
will help me live?
I stand alone.

## III

In 1929, I walked into the bar.
They called it "Bluebird" on the night
it was gay.
I heard of other gay bars,
moving locations,
using names of birds or references
to Walt Whitman's poems.

Walt Whitman, the voice of America,
beating his chest,
shouting out America's song
with pen and paper,
while belonging to
the silenced minority
in the country he celebrated.

Though seeing my name in print,
I felt nothing like a great poet
or orator
when I appeared in the paper
that next day, among the list
of "perverts" arrested
for attending a "lewd" gathering.

"Lewd"? My hands were shaking so hard,
I could barely hold onto my beer,
much less hold onto someone else
in any way…
lewd or otherwise.

Because of the "lewdness,"
I lost my job, my lease,
my family.
But I learned of others like me.

They had two choices:

stand alone,
or don't stand at all.
They chose to stand alone.
I asked myself,
since I have them,
why not stand with them?

Change took too many years,
and still comes slowly.
Soon, it was 1969.
Gay icon Judy Garland died,
and some drag queens were just
in a bad mood
when the police raided
that bar, Stonewall.
They fought back.
Rioted. In heels!

## IV

Yes, I'm gay,
but I'm not like them.
Those old queens
embarrass me.

Why are they wearing dresses?
Why are they so fey,
so fem?

We can't be normal,
can't be accepted,
if we can't look like
act like,
be like,
dress like
the ones who
want to stop us
from being ourselves.

Why can't those queens
turn into real men
and take a stand?

## V

We fought like
Palestinians and Israelis
in the Gaza strip,
Or Protestants and Catholics
in Ireland,
but we were born
of the same mother.

In adulthood,
reached with a draft card
and gun fire,
we served together.
We forgot our fights,
and the feuds between
our neighboring churches.

But I hate
that we were still fighting
someone else's brothers.

After the war,
you went back there
with your church
and helped rebuild,
seeing no enemies,
only God's children.

## VI

His faith is different from mine;
therefore, he is infidel,
nonbeliever, heretic, enemy…
the list goes on
like the battles,

the soldiers killed,
the wounded,
falling alone.
Of course I hate violence,
and want it to stop,
but I'm just one woman,
and he's a sinner.
I must take a stand
for my God.

## VII

We marched together
demanding our right to vote,
demanding that our brothers
and sisters register
for that vote.

We walked until our feet ached,
and our hand-me-down shoes
began falling apart.

We marched when
folks chanted racial slurs,
threw rocks at us,
or hosed us down,
and we kept marching
when we heard about
our brothers and sisters who died
for speaking of freedom.

We marched for you
to have a chance
at a better education,
a better life,
and so you will
never feel ashamed of
the blackness of your skin.

## VIII

Your skin is blacker
than mine.
Yes, I'm black too,
but you're too black
to make it in this world.

I'm sorry,
but that's how it is,
even in
the twenty-first century.

Lighter is better.

The sooner you realize that,
the more you can better yourself,
be yourself,
and then stand up to racism
and prove that people of color
can succeed.

## IX

After the tsunami hit,
a relief worker
pulled me up
from the rubble
of the hotel where I worked.

I couldn't stand alone,
because the broken glass
severed my leg.

I stood with her.

I don't speak English
so she couldn't ask
if I pray like her,

think like her,
love like her,
belong to the same country,
or to a country club.

Besides, I knew she didn't care
about any of that.

She didn't care
how dark I am,
how light I am,
how feminine, masculine, militant,
orthodox, radical, liberal,
conservative, young, or old,
how divided against my siblings.

I couldn't stand alone,
so I stood with her.

## X

At the pope's funeral,
you hugged me like
we were old friends.
I suppose we are,
though our people
hate each other.

You are my sibling.

Please don't wait for the next
flood, bombing, tornado, hurricane,
shooting, plague, draught, war,
outbreak, breakdown, mourning,
before you stand with me again.
We have each other.
Why stand alone?

# HOMELESS, I: CITIES DON'T BUILD PEOPLE

A shopping bag lady
with emptied dreams
remembers coming to the city
to become a star.

The phone calls never came.
No curtains rose.
No one sang her songs
or listened to her
when she sang them.
No one found a part
for her in any play.

The hotel money ran out
and the bus went east.

She left the bus station
and lives here now.

# HOMELESS, II: ALSO

Wind blows the newspapers
out the dumpster
where you search for food.

Torn clothes
pulled around a skeleton...

with so many like you,
you become the same person.
I pass, say nothing.

When you see me again,
I look away.
You continue exploring a world
I pretend not to know.

Your words fly like sparrows
across the empty parking lot,
echoing a thousand apologies.
You say my words for me.
"I'm sorry.
We can't help you."

# FAMILY

Daughter asks about
the whiteness of her skin.
Even after growing up
in the fields,
under the sun
of Vietnam,
she remains paler
than her younger
brother and sisters.

Mother says
it's nothing strange
for a child of the 60s,
the time of pale skin.
Daughter asks about
the father she never met.
Mother says he went away
and promised to return,
but died in the war,
or forgot his name,
his family.

Father looks through pictures
of his buddies from the war,
of his time in Vietnam,
thinks of his lover,
of touching her stomach
and feeling the kicking
of their child.

He never told his family,
never told the wife
he left for two years,
never told anyone
of the child he fathered
on the night

his best friend died
from friendly fire,
his friend...his fire,
the night he just needed
someone to hold him.

# Ex-Gay? Part I: Cocoon

I thought changing my life
was like picking out furniture.
You tell me to send out
for dry-clean soul service.

I came here to escape.
I came here for Bible class,
Christian CD's, Christian concerts,
Christian videos, Christian T-shirts.

I wear it all.
I hear it all.
I wrap myself up in
holy armor,
to keep from seeing
who I am.

I say the lines with you,
repeat the liturgy.
In order to keep
your unconditional love,
I never dare tell you
that I'm gay,
though I see my face in your eyes,
hear my thoughts in your voice,
wrap my secret in your hug.

We agree to the code
of silence.
We take the vow
of chastity.
We wear the mask,
walk the walk,
talk the talk,
lie the lie.

# EX-GAY? PART II: THE EX-ME MOVEMENT

They wired his genitals
and showed him pictures of naked women.
They hoped for arousal.
But then they showed him pictures of naked men.
It made him think of the other boy his age,
the one his parents caught him with.
A jolt of electricity shot through his body.

He had heard that such programs faded long ago.
He had heard of teenage boys during the Victorian era
forced to wear devices to bed,
ones that hurt circulation,
and simply hurt.
He had heard of the Nazis
conducting their cruelest experiments
on those with the pink triangle,
but this was today, and this was America.

He was in love,
and no one could shock that out of him.
The hypnosis sessions could not convince him
that he wasn't himself.

He met a lesbian who pretended to be cured.
She told him that he should wear the same mask
if he didn't want to be hated by his family
or end up on the streets,
or locked away forever.
She told him,
"It's a free country,
as long as you aren't you."
He knew what she meant.
The parents who loved him could turn
against him,
and commit this abuse,
and no one would stop them.

Everyone called it "tough love."
He saw the "tough," but not the "love."

After he escaped,
he found his way to New York City,
looked for work,
found violence and drugs.
Cold and bruised,
he went to a safe house
for teens like himself,
escapees from tough love.

Still, he must hide with the others
in these cramped quarters
for the next two years,
until he reaches legal adulthood.

He thinks of the boy he loves
and will never see again.
He thinks of the parents he loves
and will never see again.
He wonders if he should call this
"tough love."

# EX-GAY? PART III: WHO DOES GOD HATE?

Susan's hand touched Rick's back,
nearly jerking away at the same time.
She always touched him that way,
as if disarming a bomb—
afraid of making it,
or letting it,
explode.
He couldn't fake sleep anymore;
somehow, she learned to tell.

He feared she would laugh at him,
see him as less than a man,
hate him for rejecting her.
He hoped her hand
would settle between his shoulder blades,
that she would give up, fall asleep.
He wanted to hold her
like a sibling or a friend,
but not like a lover.

Her hand caressed his shoulders.
He jerked away.
He wanted to admit to using her
as part of his disguise,
his accessories,
his badge of acceptance,
his backstage pass onto
the stage of normalcy.

His parents had asked him,
"Who does God hate?"
Then they promptly
gave the answer he feared:
homosexuals.
"Homosexuals" meant him.
"God" meant their version of God.

Coming out to them
meant losing them.
He never believed God hated anyone,
but he began to think
his parents hated him,
or at least they would,
if he failed to change.

For two years, Rick went to
the Christian counselor,
who used up his college fund,
went to the "ex-gay" meetings,
with printed listings of "cured" gays,
who Rick later saw at the gay bar,
people who believed they could
pray and read a Bible verse
then turn into John Wayne.

He told his parents, "I'm cured,"
so he could hear them call him
"son"
again,
so he could escape the group
that always said,
"try harder, try harder,"
that made him want to slit his wrists.

He wanted to make himself
love Susan
the way she loved him.
Surely, if he married her,
that would fix everything.

But four years into their marriage,
he still couldn't hold her
like she held him.

Susan's hand pulled away,
And they went to sleep.

One night,
Rick finally chose the words
and told his story.
For what seemed hours,
she cried,
asking how he could use her
and lie to her that way.

But then she said she always saw it,
an image in the back of her mind,
a ghost she saw then denied,
convincing herself it could not exist.

As the days passed
and the anger subsided,
she began to see Rick,
not as ghost, lover, or husband.

She held his hand,
like a sibling, like a friend.

# SPIRAL STAIRCASE

I hold the candle
while twisting upward,
and then downward
on a spiral staircase
leading nowhere.
As the fire gives light,
the candle melts.
Where am I going?

The stairs aren't sturdy;
rust peels in my hands.
I grip the railings
and doubt their strength.

Twisting
through my house,
I see darkness,
and feel thirst.

In a house
with no lights,
I stay lost.
No one seems
to care enough
to free me.

When you get old,
people forget you.
They think someone else
went to see you,
and someone else
brought you your medication,
if they think of you at all.

My husband always wanted
a spiral staircase.

Now he's gone,
and I only want
to find my way
outside.

No home
left in my house,
no me
left in myself.
No end to these stairs.
Where am I going?

# VIOLENCE

(Author's note: I wrote two closely related essays shortly after the bombing in Oklahoma City, addressing the questions that arose around how America could survive that travesty. Here, I combine the two into a single essay. Though I never directly refer to the bombing, the feelings of that time inspired this writing.)

I would like to raise some questions and suggestions regarding how individuals can help prevent violence. Law enforcement should punish those who resort to violence, but I mean none of the following as potential laws; I bring them up only as challenges for those who wish to quell hostilities in our great nation. Our discussions of modern America usually involve more fingers pointed than solutions offered. Instead of always looking for scapegoats, we need to look for better ways to strengthen America. I offer the following approaches, though we can find countless others if we only learn to listen to one another. All of these might sound naïve or simplistic, but I honestly believe they can help. I only suggest them as ways of helping—not as easy or magical cures.

To start with, all people should stop and consider their words. Angry, bitter words add tension, instead of resolving problems. Tapping into someone else's anger can lead to constructive action, or destructive action, so we should weigh the possible outcomes before manipulating such volatile emotions.

And speaking of the words we choose, parents and other role models must teach children something basic before sending them off to school or into the world: manners. Simple terms like the following can defuse many tense situations and create an atmosphere of respect: "thank you, excuse me, pardon me, sorry, I apologize, please, ma'am, sir, may I, it's my fault, you go first." Conversely, teachers should require that students refrain from words like "nigger" and "faggot," which promote hatred, self-hatred, division, isolation, and violence. Aside from the simple use of respectful language, children need to learn to take blame and responsibility for their actions (as well as their inaction), and to show consideration for others, regardless of differences in opinion, beliefs, or anything else.

Also, we should not see terrorism or hate crimes as bravery. It takes courage to openly debate each other's views, to work for peace and justice, or to examine why we fear differences. It takes courage to admit that we might be wrong, misinformed, or uninformed. Shouting our views while plugging our ears, waving a gun, or blowing up a building takes no courage.

If some human lives matter, why not see them all as important? We must act more responsibly in our human interaction, instead of finding new ways to hate each other, new groups to hate, new excuses for violence.

Those in public life carry an even greater responsibility. With street gangs, skinheads, and other armed groups springing up all over America, could influential speakers tone down the militant rhetoric? To some people, spiritual warfare means killing those they demonize, and culture war means civil war. Often, politicians and televangelists will warn about the violent effects of songs and movies, then broadcast irresponsible messages like "We must wage war in America." Most people recognize songs and movies as fiction, but many Americans base reality on the words of religious and political leaders.

These same speakers often use particular groups as scapegoats to society's problems. Yes, it works as a fund-raising ploy, but such claims manifest themselves in threats like "They want to destroy your country and your children." Someone prone to insecurity and violence might take that not as a campaign slogan or donation request, but as an invitation to use a gun, knife, or baseball bat on the latest selections in the enemy-of-the-week club.

Leaders everywhere must realize that some people might twist their stands into a battle cry. Therefore, leaders can demonstrate their leadership skills by (1) unequivocally denouncing violence; (2) educating people in non-violent conflict resolution, including general problem-solving skills; and (3) teaching people that self-defense means fighting off a literal flesh-and-bone attack, not seeking out and attacking those someone branded as the enemy within.

All of us, as leaders, followers, or just people trying to survive, can make our lives special, exciting, and memorable, but we cannot escape the shortness and fragility of our life on Earth. Why waste that short life by creating a hostile environment?

As individuals, we might lack the ability to overcome many of the social or economic factors that lead to desperate acts for many Americans. And no amount of logic can stop the irrational hatred of terrorists and hate groups. However, individuals decide how to speak to each other and how to treat each other. We make those decisions, and we need to make them carefully every day, instead of blaming anyone or anything for how we choose to interact.

We could give ourselves the satisfaction of knowing we worked for a better, less violent society. Even with all our human imperfections and all our natural differences, we can certainly make some improvements—not Utopia, just the America we worked so hard to build. Please pray, act, and react for peace. Put down the weapons, lower the tone, and treat others as you want them to treat you.

# STORM

I hear the thunder
as drums of a past celebration.
The lightning dances
like King David
praising God.

Can we stay and laugh
in the victory march
of falling rain?

Why call this noise terrible?
The ground, the trees,
and the crops
all feed in the fury.

When the dance ends,
the colors come alive.

# THE ESCAPE ARTIST

Ann dreams hour upon hour,
stacking fantasies on her bedposts.
They maintain balance
with their fingertips,
leaping…
r
  e
    a
      c
        h
          i
            n
              g.

Trapeze artists,
tightrope walkers,
seeking adventure.
Always a hero!

Traversing a rainbow
on a butterfly!
Why set limits
for a child's dreamland?

Ann dreams hour upon hour,
while I try to remember
such dreams.

# DAUGHTER

I have been here a long time
watching your traces of childhood
fade away
like clouds changing shape.
Your favorite playground
became a shopping center.
When they laid the last brick,
the little girl was gone.

I have worked here a long time,
the same job in the same city.
As long as I could
buy you dresses, toys,
books, and pizza,
it never really mattered
where I worked, what I did.

But I wonder if you're happy
with where you work,
with who you know.
Those little girls
who made you giggle
don't wear the same ribbons.
I no longer see children,
no longer see
my precious little girl.

Your friends might leave you.
That boyfriend of yours,
the one who needs a haircut,
he might find someone else,
though I hope he doesn't.
You seem to love him.
Your job and your major
might change.
But, since your major is theater,

I might be happy about that.

But whatever changes
or doesn't change,
I'll still be here,
watching you grow,
finding shapes
in the clouds of your life,
and telling you what I see.
You might not see the same shapes.
It really doesn't matter,
as long as you still
face the sky
with wonder.

I loved that playground,
where I pushed you
on the swing
and worried about you
on the monkey bars.
You're so fragile,
but I think you were safe there,
and I really don't think
we needed another
shopping center

or another grown-up.

# THE SAME LIPS

Under your microscope,
Adam through a glass darkly,
flesh torn with steel instruments,
to expose my heart.
You want to prove it beats
differently than yours.
You want to prove it carries
some other blood.

No longer the child
in my science class,
You become the hunter,
and I become the hunted,
Adam to Adam.

Print your made-up statistics.
Tell everyone you'll save them
from me, with a donation
to your Mercedes fund.

Hide what you found:
my heart like yours,
my blood like yours,
with only a few
innate differences:
Atom to atom.

Hide your eyes
when kneeling at the altar.
Hide your eyes
from what they know.

You would never admit
you saw me pray,
inside your rifle scope:
I, the target,

I, your neighbor.
You point at the scars
left by your probing
and say I inflicted them
on myself.

# PHARISEE

I am a sail
that tore itself from the boat
it once served.

I am the colors;
I am a firework display
and a peacock.

I am a magazine cover,
a judge of fashion,
a fashionable judge.

I am a banner
announcing my own presence.

# THE LOSS

The game
complete,
he closes his bedroom eyes,
makes her go away.

## ADDING TO THE HURT

Sadly, much of the world continues to ignore the violence that many nongays commit against gays. Even certain gays perpetrate anti-gay violence. In some cases, they hope it will destroy the part of themselves they hate: their own gayness. So they attack someone outside a gay bar, or at some other location, maybe even at school. Supposedly, it will win them acceptance, the coveted and privileged heterosexual status. They often get away with the violence.

In some cases, gays who can't accept their orientation will find a gay lover but assault that lover. Many of our supporters like to point out the similarities between gay couples and male/female ones. Unfortunately, those similarities include many of the same problems.

Not long ago, because of the stigma of divorce and the difficulty of women supporting themselves, almost all victims of domestic violence would silently suffer, even at the cost of ignoring physical, verbal, and sexual abuse against their children. Nongays only recently began confronting the constant and hidden crime of domestic violence; much of it still goes unreported.

With gays, reporting might not bring results, as many self-anointed "family values" politicians and even some law enforcement officials seem to enjoy seeing gays hurt themselves and each other—if not through unsafe sex, then through some other means. They will only use bad gay relationships as an excuse to justify anti-gay laws.

Also, reporting it might mean outing oneself—a step that many gays simply might not feel ready to take. They keep their relationship quiet; the violence in the relationship also remains secret.

With such an environment, I would say the following to any gay person in a violent relationship. Quit waiting for someone to intervene. Get out of any abusive relationship; it will just get worse, no matter how many promises your partner makes. Maybe some people think you deserve physical and verbal abuse; however, the same people think you deserve AIDS, hate crimes, and discrimination, so find someone more sympathetic to give you guidance.

No one deserves a violent relationship, just as no one deserves those other tragedies. You need a loving, supportive romance, one in which two people coexist without violence or threats, regardless of their mood, self-image, job, or past companions. Hold out for a nurturing relationship, no matter how long it takes. Refuse to accept violence from anyone, even if the attacker comes back later to say "I love you."

Check your yellow pages and/or the internet for information on domestic violence prevention in your area. Find support, and stop letting loved ones push or strike you.

# BAREBACK

Louder, louder, the music pulsing
harder. Lights flashing, faster.
Young male bodies grinding harder
on the crowded dance floor,
in the ecstasy of ecstasy.
Heat, sweat, eyes, hands,
another night, pulsing faster
than crystal shooting
through your veins
harder than a stranger
in a hurry, in a daze.
Simply in. He says it's better
without.

And you think it can't happen to you,
but if it did, the new magic pills
would make it go away,
but this time it pulses faster
than crystal shooting
through your veins,

faster than insurance running out,
faster than parents walking away,
faster than friends dying off,
faster than a virus mutating,
faster than another cure failing,

faster than the thirty seconds
he wouldn't take
to open a package
and slide on a condom.

But all that happens off stage.
With perfect hair and perfect clothes,
we live in the safety of the dance floor.

Make up a name,
and tell me, do you ride
skin to skin?

# SUCCESS

This isn't the future
we wanted.

Acid rain.
Volcanoes in the sky
emit every color but green.
Where did the wind
learn this chant?

A prison,
cold and dry…
The smell of death,
the taste of hunger.

"Colonel," says the young guard.
"The prisoner's dead."

Eyes of stone
order the removal
of another lifeless body,
this one a woman
accused of speaking
forbidden thoughts.
They let her starve.
Words for the commanding officer
are weapons from the stockpile.
He finds no use for either anymore.

The prisoner had asked for paper.
The guard reclaims it,
examines the crumpled words
written while her life faded.

"Can you read English?"
asks the guard.

The colonel begins to shake his head,
but then speaks
for the first time in days.
His voice emerging tears at his throat.
"No, but keep it.
It might be important."

Despite losing her life,
the poet's greatest wish comes true…
her work lives after her.

# SPELUNKER

I see you
trapped in a cave
you ran into one day
during a storm
that threatened your home.

Angry winds
kept visiting
your stone pillow,
disrupting sleep.
After the storm passed,
you remained
in damp safety.

"No passage," you say.
"Passages lead downward,
into Earth's depths,
like following a mole."

When light invades,
you draw your eyes tighter,
even though you hate
the darkness
and isolation
of depression.

Girl in a cave,
the storm passed years ago.
Please come outside.
This dungeon needs no keeper.

# OUT OF THE CLOSET

(Author's note: I wrote this essay for a local newsletter, and as a handout for Lubbock's chapter of PFLAG.)

Coming out isn't for all gays, and we should respect their decisions about what we might call "outness," as long as they aren't attacking other gays from the safety of the closet.

However, I want to touch on some of the basics of coming out, for those who choose to take those steps. I should begin by noting that the steps can vary wildly, because gays and lesbians aren't all the same, and they aren't all in the same places (mentally or geographically). So you'll need to adapt the order or importance of these guidelines according to your situation, personality, etc.

First of all, come out to yourself. Get past the denial stage. Explore your emotions and how you identify yourself. Read some of the many excellent books from gay or gay-friendly authors.

While reading, you need to learn about yourself and your culture. Information will empower you. Lesbian and gay individuals make and have made countless contributions to Western civilization, especially in the arts. Learn about our history and what it means to you.

That might be enough for you. Some people will feel satisfied with that knowledge, and not see the need to come out any further.

If you want to come out further, though, the next step might be to come out to some gay people. You don't have to sleep with them to talk to them. Besides, sex won't answer all the questions that keep haunting you. Please get the complete facts on safer sex before getting into bed with someone. Since most schools refuse to give you the thorough, blunt, and life-saving information everyone needs about AIDS and other STD's, you can get it from gay activists or the many health care workers who reach out to the gay community.

Besides safer sex guidance, you also need a lot of other information, as well as a support base. Rely on the various groups listed in your local (or nearest) gay community newsletter, and find resources via the internet.

Still, please keep the following in mind: just as some blacks might not like a particular black organization or some Christians might not like a particular Christian organization, you might encounter a gay organization that you dislike. Don't let that dissuade you from trying others. I strongly suggest PFLAG's meetings or Web site (http://www.pflag.org).

Who else can you come out to? Some people just wave a rainbow flag on TV, or come out in a classroom, but please weigh the possible outcomes before trying anything sudden, daring, or dangerous. Most people seem to find it easier to come out away from their hometown, maybe at a gay pride parade or maybe just to a nongay friend. When heterosexuals realize they know and like a gay person, it usually becomes harder for them to see us as monsters that they should hunt down and destroy.

What about your family? Not if you still rely on them financially, unless you know for sure that your disclosure won't affect those finances, or unless you know you can survive without their money. Not on a holiday; whatever the original purpose of the holiday, it probably involves a lot of tension now, and adding to the tension might lead to words everyone will regret. Not to everyone at once; take the most understanding one aside, then plan how to proceed from there. Not out of anger or spite; think of and explain gayness as simply part of your existence, not as something you do to your parents. Not if it might put you in physical danger or put you in a situation where an argument could lead to severed family ties.

If needed, write a letter to your family. You might come across as too bitter or confrontational in the letter's first draft, so make sure you set it aside for a while before revising it; besides, the writing and revising process will allow you to sort through your feelings. You need to deal with that anger—better now than during an already difficult conversation.

What about your job? You'll need to decide for yourself if you should come out at work. It depends on your occupation, location, coworkers, and boss.

Whatever approach seems best for you and your situation, why not start the coming-out process? Plan it out, instead of rushing into it blindly. Talk to gays and their parents about what works and what to avoid. Get informed, then decide the best steps to take.

# THE JOHN DOE FAMILY

Lightning dives
into a sea of green.
The limb imposes;
the roof accepts our guest.
No, I heard nothing.

Sleep, gentle children;
all is well.

The scream of the impact
replied to the thunder,
and they conspire
to drown us in our home.
But FBI man won't find us;
New World Order won't force you
into their brainwash schools,
or force us
to pay their taxes.

Sleep, gentle children;
all is well.

Dream of tomorrow,
playing
in the fall-out shelter,
a new game of hide and seek;
no one will be the searcher
as we hide forever.
This game will be our favorite.

# FAMILY REUNION

The holidays. Time for sharing with your relatives. Time to bring home the spouse and the kids. Or maybe not. Gays and lesbians might encounter one of the scenarios that follow.

The holidays. Time to lie to your relatives and yourself. Time to refer to your beloved as a roommate, if anything at all. Time to play heterosexual, so as not to cause a ruckus in nice Christian homes. Time to hear the relationships of your relatives receive acknowledgment, amid comments about homophobic legislation saving America.

The holidays. Time to look for an open restaurant, because you tried honesty with your parents, because you bought into their "unconditional love" rhetoric, only to learn of the heterosexual clause in that contract. They responded, "I never want to see you again. How could you do that to us? How could you choose that lifestyle? You'll burn in Hell. Get out, so we can sing another refrain of 'And they'll know we are Christians by our love.'"

The holidays. Time to face the awkward blend of accepting, uninformed, and ambivalent relatives. "Now, let's see," says your lover. "Your grandma knows, and she marched in the gay pride parade. Your parents are okay with it, as long as we don't touch. Your oldest brother thinks it's disgusting. Your two sisters might know. Aunt Jessie would just die. Never mind. I'll just pet the gay-friendly dog."

The holidays. This time, you visit your lover's folks. Both sets of parents acknowledge your relationship just as they would that of a male/female couple, understanding that all human beings share a capacity for love. On their wall, you see a picture of you and your partner holding hands. You hear relatives say they're writing Congress to complain about anti-gay legislation, because it unfairly targets their loved ones.

The holidays. You volunteer at the nearest AIDS outreach, or other places that help those in need. You create your own traditions. You find the acceptance and sense of family you need, in an environment where pretense falls away, in favor of love.

# A GREAT AMERICAN VOICE

Many people consider Anne Bradstreet (1612–1672) the first American poet. She was definitely the first woman in America with a published book. A Puritan woman who lived with her husband in New England, she faced and chronicled numerous hardships, leaving behind an inspirational body of poetry.

Bradstreet admitted to embarrassment over her success, but none of her critics—and she was perhaps her greatest critic—could stop her from becoming one of America's most influential authors. Her words and her life inspired me to write the following dedication.

Visit Web sites such as annebradstreet.com to learn more about this extraordinary author. Collections of her work include *The Works of Anne Bradstreet, To My Husband and Other Poems*, and *Tenth Muse*.

# ANNE BRADSTREET

Tear into her pages.
Devour her manuscript.
Render her words
in your tone,
but you can't forget
Anne's voice
of early America.

Already published,
her book
learns to evade
fireplaces,
forgotten shelves.

# CYCLE

Wedding bells faded
Into the alarm clock's scream
And the test results.

You laughed and embraced,
Smiling as you both trembled
And stared beyond youth.

On a spring morning,
Tiny hands began to move,
Waving at the light.

Blue eyes soon faded
Through tears of confusion;
"Why does Daddy leave?"

From Mt. Sinai's peak
I carried that report card;
Your eyes were medals.

"Daddy won't be home."
I became so much younger,
Crying, screaming, scared.

Headlights passed me like
Searchers in the parking lot;
I hid from all lights.

Over time I became
As absent as my father.
He left; I stole, and

That is how I found
Myself in jail at nineteen,
Instead of college.

Your hands reached out through
The rusting bars and questions
When I made you cry.

Kate helped me each day
With her visits…a good friend
Who would become more.

She accepted my
Hand in marriage, but we lacked
A home for our plans.

"Really, Mom, just once."
You paid the rent and somehow
I kept that promise.

Kate graduated
Alongside our son, Thomas,
Oldest in her class.

I wish you had seen
Tom accept his doctorate;
Kate's eyes were medals.

Dad finally met
His grandchild before he died.
I treasured our time,

And he cried, asking
If I could forgive him, but
I already had.

Still teaching part-time,
I forget my age and see
Eyes staring beyond youth.

# CROSS

A young man, about twenty,
Hair long, like the sixties,
Pimples lingering, like the seventies,
Lives in my college dorm,
Three doors away,
The door that says,
"Ask me about Jesus,"
The door that says,
"Choose God or Choose Hell."

He has lived there, so close,
More than a year,
Wearing T-shirts that turn
Liquor ads and rock bands
Into commercial gospel tracts,

As if I could buy God
At the corner liquor store
Between brown bottles
Of Tennessee whiskey
And the latest football/beer
Tie-in sweepstakes,
As if the music department
Of the dollar store
Offered salvation
At a bargain price,
Rain checks available.

The commercial evangelist
In my dorm complex
Looks the other way
When I walk by.

The commercial evangelist
With the messiah complex
Writes angry letters

To the school paper
Condemning everyone
But himself.

He never speaks to me
About Jesus or the weather.
He passes me every day,
Never returning my "hello."

He retreats to his room,
His sacred ground.
He turns up his stereo,
Plays Christian heavy metal,
Sings along.

# HERO

That is my banner
Displayed in the fires
That burn women and children.
The death count goes down
With so few left to die.

The survivors salute me,
Hold my picture
Against their bloodied faces
As they march through the wreckage
Without recognizing
The charred skeletons of their homes
Or families.

These human lives
Sewn into a pattern
Like rags I can spare
Fall into the desert sand
That once bore life,
Before I transformed it
Into a graveyard,
For which I received medals.

Some of the dead children
Were probably named after me.
We follow the rivers of blood by day
And the burning crops by night.
Lungs filled with ashes,
I cannot give another speech.

# TWO RAPES

He holds the knife
To her throat,

Says, "You need it baby.
You need a man.
So you won't want no women
No more. I'll give you
What you need, baby.
I'll give you
What they can't give."

He invades her,
Tears her open
Like a can of beer
He'll empty then toss aside,
Repeating, "It's what you need."

Judge-man hands the rapist
A one-month sentence,
Looks at the victim as if to say,
"He was only giving you
What you need, baby."

# IF: A SATIRE

(Note to the humor-impaired: this is a satire. Please don't use it to represent my views. Please don't shoot anyone. Please don't call your lawyer while sticking your finger into a light socket. Please don't eat three hundred hamburgers while complaining that fast food makes you fat. Please don't use your hairdryer in the shower. Thank you. You may now proceed.)

As a Christian, I love fags, though they're degenerates who we must silence, deny civil rights, and fire from their jobs. Homosexuality occurs in many animals, which means it's unnatural. If God wanted gay people, He would have created Adam and Steve.

Were Adam and Eve a multi-racial couple? If not, why do so many races exist today? If God wanted more than one race, He would have created Achmed and Eve.

Were Adam and Eve blind? Maybe blind people choose not to see. If God wanted blind people, why did He give us eyes?

Were Adam and Eve mentally or physically handicapped? Maybe so-called "disabled people" just want special rights, or just want to cause trouble for us normal people. Maybe, as many good Christians believe, God is punishing them or their parents for sin or lack of faith.

Were Adam and Eve epileptic? Maybe demons possess epileptics, like the Bible says. Maybe they choose to have seizures—as some perverted, anti-social behavior—then dare to call it biologically pre-determined. Surveys prove that epileptics have a secret agenda to destroy America and outlaw flashing lights.

Was Adam or Eve left-handed? If Adam were left-handed and Eve right-handed, wouldn't that mean God wants all men to rely on their left hands and all women to rely on their right hands? Since the majority is right-handed, left-handedness signals perversity, as we believed in more godly times.

Were Adam and Eve co-pilots? If God wanted people to fly, He would have given them wings. The Bible never mentions airplanes because God never intended for us to use them, just like electricity and all the other inventions that keep us from being like Adam and Eve. I'll use my semi-automatic rifle on anyone who tries to make me use any invention not invented directly by God. The fact that many people are banning peanuts on airline flights only shows how dangerous they are.

Were Adam and Eve murderers? If they were, they might have killed each other before they had a chance to have Cain, who killed Abel. Obviously, the

Bible doesn't want us to start killing people until we have a few extra breeders around to spare.

Were Adam and Eve sterile? If we start accepting sterility, humanity will die out. So should we not see sterile people as a threat to society? They can only have babies through unnatural, scientific means, and we all know that science comes from Charles Darwin and his master, Satan. Since babies made by science don't come from God, they don't have souls. Anyone who can't help being sterile shouldn't copulate, because copulation is only for reproduction.

We should outlaw birth control, for the same reason. Any sexual act that can't lead to children is unnatural and ungodly. If God wanted Adam to use a condom, He would have given him one, and we wouldn't be here, but you probably never even thought of that, because you don't have the understanding that only comes from God.

I have that understanding. God's the one who told me to write this ordained essay and told you to read it. How does it feel following God's will and sharing God's love for a change, you demonic slug? I'm going to laugh when you burn in Hell with the people I've been talking about.

But I don't condemn anyone. I just let God speak through me. What you're reading is God talking. He doesn't always use King James English, you know. I'm just speaking His truth in love, the only truth. But I'm sorry for digressing when your unenlightened mind already has trouble receiving the complex message of God's love.

What about perverts who say a dog is man's best friend? Genesis says God created woman as man's companion. Hunters use dogs to help them kill animals, which directly links the violent crime crisis to dog lovers. If God wanted a dog as man's best friend, He would have created Adam and Spot.

Rednecks? Bubba and Eve. Political parties? Adam Bush and Eve Clinton. Denominations? Adam Luther and Eve Calvin.

Did Adam and Eve eat pizza, hamburgers, or tacos? Did they use money, microwaves, lawnmowers, computers, or medicine? Did they pay taxes, interest, admission, tuition, tithes, tips, or insurance? Did they have a wedding ceremony? Did they expect their children to marry outside their immediate family?

Obviously, Genesis mentions none of the above. Therefore, I consider it all sinful, and a threat to family values. Statistics show it all causes earthquakes, meteors, tornadoes, drive-by shootings, ozone depletion, ear-biting athletes, presidential hanky panky, sexual harassment in the military, and global warming.

Those who seek to destroy the holy institutions of discrimination and money-grubbing TV evangelists deserve none of the same rights as those of us who want to uphold the Constitution and share God's love. According to some highly reliable sources, it has been said that it is a known, true fact that expert scientific evidence proves that we must stop them, before they get us kicked out of the Garden of Eden.

# THE BIBLE AND GAYS

(Author's note: I adapted this essay from three separate but overlapping ones that appeared in the first edition of *Holding Me Together*. I had originally written one of those essays as a hand-out for Lubbock's chapter of PFLAG. Though it covers some of the same material as "Reactions to Homophobia," its brevity makes it a quick reference.)

"And Ruth said [to Naomi], Entreat me not to leave thee, or to return from following after thee: for whither thou goest, I will go; and whither thou lodgest, I will lodge: thy people shall be my people, and thy God my God: Where thou diest, will I die, and there will I be buried: the Lord do so to me, and more also, if aught but death part thee and me" (Ruth 1:16–17).

"I am distressed for thee, my brother Jonathan: very pleasant hast thou been unto me: thy love to me was wonderful, passing the love of women" (II Samuel 1:26).

"Every man shall kiss his lips that giveth a right answer" (Proverbs 24:26).

God gave us each other for companionship (Genesis 2:18). Certain people need to reproduce, but not everyone (Matthew 19:12; I Corinthians 7:1–8). The Creation accounts never mention gays as part of God's Creation, but they also never mention the disabled or the different races. Besides two passages that sound like gay relationships (Ruth 1:16–17; II Samuel 1:26), most people who object to homosexuality would probably rather not visualize John 13:5; Proverbs 24:26; I Samuel 18:1–5; II Samuel 20:3–4, 16–18, 33–34.

"Behold, this was the iniquity of thy sister Sodom, pride, fullness of bread, and abundance of idleness was in her and in her daughters, neither did she strengthen the hand of the poor and needy" (Ezekial 16:49).

The Bible blames the destruction of Sodom and Gomorrah on wickedness, greed, callousness, and inhospitably (Genesis 14–19; Ezekial 16:49; Mark 6:11; Matthew 10:14). Only sheer inventiveness can force "wicked" to mean "gay." God decides to destroy the cities, but says He will spare them for ten good men. After God's decision, some men say they want to "know" the visiting angels; somehow, that part of the Sodom passages will become the basis for using the entire story against gays, as if all the people (including the babies) of both cities are gay.

Depending on which translation we use, the Bible contains three-twelve apparent condemnations involving male/male sex, one involving female/female sex, and around 360 involving male/female sex. Many Bible scholars say most of the male/male passages actually condemn rape or temple prostitution, but that the biases of translators warp them into anti-gay references. Remember that the nomadic Hebrews desperately needed children to replace those killed from battles, draughts, and slavery; they condemned all forms of birth control and understood very little about human sexuality.

Leviticus says not to eat fruit from a young tree (19:23), read horoscopes (19:26), get a haircut (19:27), get a beard trim (19:27), get a tattoo (19:28), eat shellfish (11:9–12), eat meat with fat or blood (3:17), crossbreed cattle (19:19), plant two different kinds of seed in the same field (19:19), wear clothing of mixed fabric (19:19), eat pork (11:7–8), or touch pigskin (11:8, so much for football). It also condemns gay male sex twice, once calling it an "abomination." However, Leviticus 20:25 shows Levitical use of the word "abomination" to only mean vulgar or not kosher.

The Bible also says not to use profanity (Colossians 3:8), get drunk (Proverbs 20:1), pray aloud in public (Matthew 6:1–8), swear (Matthew 5:34), call someone worthless or a fool (Matthew 5:22), or charge interest to poor people (Ex. 22:25). It demands the death penalty for using God's name in vain (Leviticus 24:16), having pre-marital sex (Deuteronomy 22:13–21), a son acting stubbornly or rebelliously (Deuteronomy 21:18–21), and children cursing their parents (Leviticus 20:9). The death penalty for adultery (Leviticus 20:10) could include a divorced person who remarries (Matthew 5:32, 19:9; Mark 10:11–12). Paul gives two lists that condemn every person ever born (Romans 1; I Corinthians 6:10), but clever uses of ellipses can make those lists only condemn gays.

With selective reading, the Bible also sanctions slavery (Ephesians 6:5; Leviticus 25:44–46), allows men concubines or multiple wives (II Samuel 5:13; I Kings 11:3; II Chronicles 11:21; Deuteronomy 21:15), bans the disabled from worship services (Leviticus 21:18–23), and establishes negative views of women (Exodus 21:7; Leviticus 12:1–8, 15:19–33, 20:18; I Corinthians 11:5, 14:34; I Timothy 2:9–15).

"But avoid foolish questions, and genealogies, and contentions, and strivings about the law; for they are unprofitable and vain" (Titus 3:9).

"For whosoever shall call upon the name of the Lord shall be saved" (Romans 10:13).

"There is neither Jew nor Greek, there is neither bond nor free, there is neither male nor female: for ye are all one in Christ Jesus" (Galatians 3:28).

See also Matthew 7:1–5, 23:5–6, 23:24; Luke 18:10–14; Colossians 3:8–14; Romans 2:1–3, 7:6, 13:8–10, 14:10–13; I Corinthians 7:6, 7:25; Galatians 3:28; Hosea 1:2; Titus 3:9–11; all of I John.

Fortunately, salvation comes simply from accepting Jesus as Lord and Savior (John 3:16–17; Romans 10:13), not from laws, literalism, or appearances of holiness.

Some people of faith will say the verses I list here are irrelevant, especially if these verses happen to be the ones that those people violate. But the verses someone else violates are, of course, all important. What convenient theology!

Coming from a Christian fundamentalist background, I know all too well how people like to pick and choose Bible verses to use against each other. Unfortunately, that promotes nothing but division and condemnation, helping no one.

If you're a Christian, please focus on the Bible's overall messages: faith, hope, love, compassion, salvation. We miss those when we pick and choose out-of-context verses to use against each other. I pray that God will teach us all to love each other, instead of warping the Bible into yet another excuse for hatred, violence, exclusion, and alienation.

# TONIGHT'S WIND

Tumbling beer cans
strike the sides
of the subway tunnel.

The letters from home
blow away.

You buy stock
against advice,
clinging to markets
with no promise,
quickly forgotten,
a testimony of ashes
like the home fire.

# DENIAL

A synthetic bag
For packaging purposes only.
Not for using as a toy;
Not for wearing as a mask.

# UNDETECTED

As the storms
fade into one,
I learn to hear the rain,
learn to taste the wind.

Now the sky
proves that sunlight
can choose to exist
within a single cloud.

As I turn,
I hear my name,
just from my mouth,
just in my mind.
Then I learn
to hear your name,
not just my own.

As the storms
fade into one,
I learn to walk outside.

# ELEPHANT ON AN OPERA STAGE

You read your program schedule
and ask me to leave.

I don't belong here.

The thunder of my footsteps
echoes too loudly
for your establishment.

You call me a stupid beast.

Even with my size,
I manage to retreat
back into the shadows.

# DETOUR

During our first trip
to Dallas together,
we see same-sex couples
walk through the gay neighborhood,
Cedar Springs,
holding hands,
and laughing.

We see rainbow stickers
in the shops and on the cars.

We see images
that admit we can love.

I introduce you,
not as my roommate,
but as my lover,
my boyfriend.

We skip the masquerade,
wear no masks,
carry no shields
to make us invisible.

The last night,
as we leave Cedar Springs,
and walk towards our car
holding hands,
I hear someone scream
"Faggots!"

Over the weekend,
I have forgotten
the voice of hatred,
but now it makes itself known.

I still hold your hand.
The voice grows smaller,
and I refuse to let it
scare me from you.

# EDITING

A pink triangle sewn to his shirt,
he walks into the gas chamber,
breathes the same air
breathed by those we remember.

History books omit this page.
Newsreels skip this frame.
Teachers tell us,
"The Nazis killed millions:
Jews, Poles, Gypsies, Jehovah's Witnesses,
and others."
But those teachers will never identify
"and others" as gays.

I am "and others."
I am "etc."

He died there, one of thousands,
thousands of "and others."
He deserves a better title.

Those who try to restore
the page, the frame, the lesson,
hear the cry…
"promoting that lifestyle,"
as if he chose his sentence,
as if gay men in Columbia chose
to become targets of the death squads,
as if men and women in Iran or Cuba
chose to receive the death sentence
for who they love,
as if a series of gay men in Texas
chose their own brutal murders,
chose for a Texas politician to say
they deserve it, and we shouldn't care,

as if American employees and tenants
choose to fear the words,
"You are not our kind. Get out!"

as if another teenager
chooses to hear the words
"You are not our child. Get out!"

I promote the need for that child
to remember "and others."

# MORE ABOUT THE AUTHOR AND HIS WORKS

Duane Simolke (pronounced "Dwain Smoky") was born in New Orleans, Louisiana, on May 28, 1965. He writes and co-writes books at his home in Lubbock, Texas.

*The Acorn Stories*. Find these tales and more in Duane Simolke's West Texas story cycle. "Flip, Turn": A different scene from the narrator's amusing but unproductive life comes to him every time he turns to swim in the opposite direction. "Survival": A young teacher (both deaf and gay) clashes with his school's emphasis of uniformity over diversity and sports over academics. "Knock": A father sees his daughter abandon her Mexican heritage, and he now fears other types of abandonment. "Mae": Standing by her husband's grave, an elderly woman looks back at the joys and challenges of marriage and motherhood. "Mirrors: A Blackmail Letter": The gay owner of an art gallery becomes the target of a "family values" witch-hunt, spear-headed by Acorn's closeted and supposedly "ex-gay" mayor.

*The Acorn Gathering: Writers Uniting Against Cancer*. Duane Simolke edited and co-wrote this fiction collection, which also features original stories by Jan Chandler, Shawna Chandler, Huda Orfali, Timothy Morris Taylor, and Bill Wetzel. Starting with characters and settings from Simolke's collection *The Acorn Stories*, this stand-alone spin-off takes readers across several landscapes, during times of trouble, change, hope, and triumph. *The Acorn Gathering* is not a cancer book, but rather a unique fiction collection, with all royalties going to the American Cancer Society!

*Degranon: A Science Fiction Adventure*. This revised version of Duane Simolke's first novel, *Degranon*, features more gay characters and a sharper focus on diversity themes. On the planet Valchondria, no illness exists, gay marriage is legal, and everyone is a person of color. However, a group called "the Maintainers" carefully monitors everyone's speech, actions, and weight; the Maintainers also force so-called "colorsighted" people to hide their ability to see in color. Taught not to think for themselves, the youth become pawns in a Degran invasion.

*The Return of Innocence*. When Sasha Varov left the land of the exiles to buy seeds in the kingdom of Jaan, she stumbled into a series of misadventures that ended with the death of the evil sorcerer Wuhrlock and made Sasha a legend, known as "Innocence." Never mind that the legend bears little resemblance to the truth or that Sasha caught Wuhrlock in an unguarded moment; the people of Jaan now expect Innocence to defeat Wuhrlock's brother, who is much more powerful. She will find allies, and adventure. Co-written with Toni Davis, from a short story Simolke wrote in 1983. This comical fantasy might not be available yet; see DuaneSimolke.Com for details.

*Stein, Gender, Isolation, and Industrialism: New Readings of Winesburg, Ohio* re-visits the best-known work of the influential American writer Sherwood Anderson. This book served as the doctoral dissertation of Duane Simolke at Texas Tech University. Dr. Simolke examines Sherwood Anderson's *Winesburg, Ohio*, as it relates to Gertrude Stein, gender roles, gay subtext, failed communication, and the machine in the garden. DuaneSimolke.Com features extensive Sherwood Anderson links and Gertrude Stein links.

Simolke also wrote the foreword to Ronald L. Donaghe's gay novel *Lance: The Continuing Journals of Will Barnett*.

Majoring in English, Simolke received degrees from Belmont University (B.A., 1989), Hardin-Simmons University (M.A., 1991), and Texas Tech University (Ph.D., 1996). StoneWall Society (http://www.stonewallsociety.com/) gave him Pride in the Arts literary awards for his books *The Acorn Stories, Degranon*, and *Holding Me Together*. His writing has appeared in dozens of publications, including *The International Journal On World Peace, nightFire, Midwest Poetry Review, Perception, Caprock Sun*, and *The New Voice of Nebraska*, as well as on Web sites such as This Week in Texas (http://www.thisweekintexas.com/).

Visit DuaneSimolke.Com for more details about Duane Simolke's books, and for related links. That site also includes Rainbow: Lubbock, Simolke's online newsletter for Lubbock gays.

978-0-595-36673-0
0-595-36673-2